TRANSFORMING
TEXTS

TRANSFORMING TEXTS

Classical Images in New Contexts

Edited by
Robert P. Metzger

Lewisburg
Bucknell University Press
London and Toronto: Associated University Presses

© 1993 by Associated University Presses, Inc.

All rights reserved. Authorization to photocopy items for internal or personal use, or the internal or personal use of specific clients, is granted by the copyright owner, provided that a base fee of $10.00, plus eight cents per page, per copy is paid directly to the Copyright Clearance Center, 27 Congress Street, Salem, Massachusetts 01970. [0-8387-5216-0/93 $10.00+8¢ pp, pc.]

Associated University Presses
440 Forsgate Drive
Cranbury, NJ 08512

Associated University Presses
25 Sicilian Avenue
London WC1A 2QH, England

Associated University Presses
P.O. Box 338, Port Credit
Mississauga, Ontario
Canada L5G 4L8

The paper used in this publication meets the requirements of the American National Standard for Permanence of Paper for Printed Library Materials Z39.48-1984.

Library of Congress Cataloging-in-Publication Data

Transforming texts : classical images in new contexts / edited by Robert P. Metzger.
   p. cm.
Includes bibliographical references and index.
ISBN 0-8387-5216-0
  1. Meaning (Philosophy)   I. Metzger, Robert P. (Robert Paul), 1937– .
B105.M4T73   1992
121'.68—dc20   91-58592
                                                                        CIP

PRINTED IN THE UNITED STATES OF AMERICA

CONTENTS

Acknowledgments	7
Introduction ROBERT P. METZGER	9
Exhibition at the Center Gallery, Bucknell University, March 14–April 29, 1987 VARUJAN BOGHOSIAN	17
1. Meaning in Native American Astronomy Texts ANTHONY F. AVENI	41
2. Boghosian on Boghosian VARUJAN BOGHOSIAN	54
3. Rambo and the Myth of Redemption ROBERT JEWETT and JOHN LAWRENCE	63
4. "It Was Ulysses and It Was Not": Traditional Refractions JOHN WHEATCROFT	84

ACKNOWLEDGMENTS

I want to extend both my personal and professional gratitude to the distinguished symposium participants: Anthony Aveni, Varujan Boghosian, Robert Jewett, John Lawrence, and John Wheatcroft. My thanks go as well to Vice President Larry Shinn, project director for planning of the National Endowment for the Humanities grant, Joseph LaBarge, chairman, Department of Religion at Bucknell University, who served as chairman of the Humanities Coordinating Council, and to the hard working members of that council: Marianna Archambault, Mary Devereaux, Joseph Fell, Pauline Fletcher, Robert Gainer, James Heath, Jackson Hill, John Murphy, Mark Neuman, Paul Noguchi, Rosalyn Richards, and Elaine Williams. This committee's rare combination of intelligence, tact, efficiency, and wisely flexible adherence to the topic made the transformation from symposium to manuscript possible. Much credit goes to Tasha Cooper, whose diligent work on a myriad of coordinating details enabled the project to move forward. Special mention must be made of the great generosity of Joel Mallin, whose loan of key works by Varujan Boghosian made the exhibition in the Center Gallery of Bucknell University a brilliant success. Photos of these works richly adorn this volume. Finally, the National Endowment for the Humanities, which is a federal agency, deserves acknowledgment for significantly contributing to the growth and productive exchange of humanistic ideas within the Bucknell community and throughout the region of central Pennsylvania.

INTRODUCTION

ROBERT P. METZGER

The significant texts from literature, art, philosophy, religion, and science, which have made lasting contributions to human life and thought, are capable of undergoing many transformations. In this sense, they share the transcendent dimension of the ancient gods for whom metamorphosis was a time-honored way of life. By transforming themselves, the gods became the archetypal embodiment of a wide range of choices available to the perceptive imagination. They served to energize, renew, and expand every subsequent epoch with their creative solutions to difficult situations and impossible challenges. They provided a continuity with the past and a bridge to the future for Western civilization. The nexus between great texts and the ancient gods is the tenacious probing for deeper significance exemplified by the incessant search for an expression of the intensification of awareness and meaning. This connection establishes the fact that the past (as an historical document) changes as rapidly as the present, and it is the past as it looks today that concerns us. The broad implication of this is that the present, which contains the past, expands in dimension by its deepening relation with the past.

The "classic" texts are the end result of the labor of human genius and as such they have transformed the world. In so doing they transform and transfigure themselves, despite the unaccountable vicissitudes of taste from age to age. It is a tribute to their sustaining transformative efficacy that these texts continue to be of concern in the late twentieth century. With the twenty-first century a little less than a decade away, the idea of a new era of empty cloning, as illustrated in the mindless electronic media, has itself become a cliché. No greater proof of the durability and potency of the classic texts is the fact of their survival in an age characterized by the pervasive mutations of standardized and synthetic values.

The collection of essays in this volume is the result of a National Endowment for the Humanities sponsored faculty planning group which met at Bucknell University in the summer of 1986. The group formulated the idea of presenting four humanities papers which, in due course, became the Transforming Texts Symposium. In the fall of that year, the group refined its ideas and urged an extension of working with the texts in two fundamental ways: defining liberal arts to include the sciences and giving emphasis to the fact that texts extend beyond the written form into the visual realm. This resulted in their invitation to the individuals whose papers were presented at Bucknell in the spring of 1987, together with an exhibition in the Center Gallery. The present volume is composed of revisions of the original presentations together with illustrations selected from the concurrent exhibition.

Among the late twentieth-century thinkers who have reformulated and resolutely transformed texts are the five whose papers are included in this volume. Two are themselves artists: poet, novelist, and essayist John Wheatcroft and visual artist Varujan Boghosian, whose work illustrates this collection. In addition, Anthony Aveni is an astronomer and archaeologist, Robert Jewett a theologian and historian, and John Lawrence a philosopher and critic. The latter two collaborated on their essay. All five had contributed decisively to a positive and thoughtful expansion of the world we inhabit through their pursuit of elementary or universal truth.

In exploring their disparate disciplines, these modern classicists have challenged conventional orthodoxies and brought to bear a rare unity with the diversity of texts they have examined. In their focused probings they have transformed the aesthetic, spiritual, scientific, and philosophical disposition of their texts for a technologically advanced age which is, ironically, in danger of intellectual default. They propose a counterview of man which stresses an awakening of our somnolent potential for inert creativity in a rejuvenated world expanded by the concepts of Marshall McLuhan's "global village" and André Malraux's "museum without walls."

Each paper has an individual viewpoint, although the writers attempted to suppress personal qualities in the execution process in order to faithfully render the truth or essence of the original text. In this way, they avoided the random, undirected, or haphazard style which often accompanies such self-determined endeavors. The writers had no concern for merely embellishing the objective treatment of their texts, but managed to avoid prescribed ways of dealing with them, achieving a balance and stability in their conclusions. The ideas presented are open-minded, suggestive, and enormously rich in possibilities, yet they bear the unmistakable imprint of the classical order of great art and civilization. They eschew the redundant, fortuitous, or inessential to set new standards for scholarly and creative achievement.

The diversity and breadth of interest and intent among the four papers presented in the original Symposium is remarkable. However, all are rooted in ancient texts whether in the Homeric poetry of Ulysses (John Wheatcroft), the Greek myth of Orpheus (Varujan Boghosian), Old Testament archetypes (Robert Jewett and John Lawrence), or the Mayan astronomers of pre-Columbian Mexico (Anthony Aveni).

Anthony Aveni has reexamined the Mayan Indian texts of ancient Mexico concerned with astronomy. In an area of study called archaeoastronomy, he has combined the disciplines of astronomy and archaeology with on-site field work. By decoding the ancient written texts, he has revealed the astronomical history of the Mayan Indians and provided links between this history and their calendar, architecture, and religion. These texts present a synthesis of religious and scientific principles and ideas quite unlike anything in Western literature. Aveni has pointed out that not only were the Maya deeply involved in observing the world around them, but they attempted to interpret the larger, hidden universe through investigations into astronomy. Despite the fact that many of the written Mayan texts have been lost, archaeoastronomy has begun to piece together bits of information which present a fuller understanding of their complex civilization. The architectural edifices which remain have further served as a text that enables contemporary scientists to broaden their fundamental research. Aveni's systematic, scientific study of the Mayan culture has been given heightened significance in light of contemporary astronomical discoveries.

A leading American artist for the past thirty years, Varujan Boghosian has evocatively adapted the classical mode to both the spirit and form of his work. Taking ancient Greek mythology as a starting point, he creates poetic, mysterious objects which exquisitely juxtapose seemingly unrelated images. By using real "found objects" such as anchor blocks, antique toys, utensils, old paintings and their stretchers, he builds nostalgic fantasies in the form of the object montage and the relief montage. The mood of surreal reverie, which these and his work in paper collage evoke, is invariably tinged with melancholy, ambiguity, and a haunting multiplicity of meaning. The discarded fragments and decorative scraps, infused by the artist with a disquieting enchantment, possess the elusive quality of a dream just beyond the edge of recollection. Boghosian is an inspired assemblage-maker who transforms the classics by providing fleeting visual clues which open the mind to free association within an explicitly literary context. This retrieval of myth and history is achieved by selecting, arranging, constructing, and thus reusing "old" material. His objects reveal the nature of the gods to the modern mind, enriching and augmenting the timeless quality of their ancient meaning. He accomplishes this dazzling metamorphosis with an imagination of such depth and power that the familiar myth of Orpheus is reborn with a freshness of vision which reverberates to our own time and place.

Robert Jewett and John Lawrence have traced the reemergence of the Biblical super-hero and hostage stories in the contemporary mass-culture film persona of "Rambo" as portrayed by Sylvester Stallone. They have pointed out the ingredients of the Rambo prototype which include varying measures of gratuitous violence, fascism, sexism, fanatic militarism, jingoism, nationalism, patriotism, and racism. They have drawn parallels between Rambo and Biblical mythic models such as the giving of the law on Mount Sinai, Moses' parting of the Red Sea and the exodus of the Jews from Egyptian bondage. Additional analogies are drawn between Rambo and Homer's *Odyssey* and Virgil's *Aeneid* as well as American portrayals of Indian captivity and bondage such as the mid nineteenth-century anonymous painting *The*

Murder of Jane McCrea and Horatio Greenough's sculpture group, *The Rescue*. All of these literary and artistic portrayals, from the Old Testament through *Rambo*, are embodied in the contemporary ritualized depictions of captivity and ransom on television news programs and the popular print media.

The ancient Homeric myth of Ulysses or Odysseus and its subsequent literary reincarnations is the focus of John Wheatcroft's study. In the ancient Greek myth, Ulysses was incessantly moving from place to place, a fact that prefigured his literary journey from the ninth century B.C. to the twentieth century A.D. Ulysses was altered by each author, beginning with Virgil, who changed Homer's hero into a villain, and then subsequently by Chaucer, Shakespeare, Dante, and Tennyson. These transformations continued into the twentieth century with Wallace Stevens's "The World of Meditation" and John Wheatcroft's own poem "The Return." Despite all of these creative celebrations and modifications, Ulysses essentially remains Homer's original. Yet, as Wheatcroft points out, he is not the same in our own time, for weariness and disillusionment weigh heavily upon him in the wake of Auschwitz, Hiroshima, and the catastrophe of World War II. Wheatcroft's poem "The Return" brilliantly interweaves the dilemma of man in the late twentieth century with the transcending myth of Ulysses. In placing Ulysses in an entirely new context and meaning, Wheatcroft enriches the ancient myth with a fresh beauty and deep profundity. Separated by a dark profusion of years, the reciprocity between Homer and Wheatcroft is nevertheless authentically and luminously felt.

The writers in this anthology have reopened kaleidoscopic portals of the past in a language common to all humanity. They have presented contemplative, insightful overtones of the past in order to make us all a little more aware of the infinite possibilities of the present. Our organs of perception would atrophy without change and diversity. When the nature and quality of stimulus to the brain is appreciably altered, each individual personality is able to grow into his or her full organic complexity. In avoiding any absolutes of method, category, or sensation, their discerning, fluid ideas of perceptual awareness resonate with echoes of intellect transformed and expanded.

TRANSFORMING
TEXTS

EXHIBITION AT THE CENTER GALLERY,
BUCKNELL UNIVERSITY,
MARCH 14–APRIL 29, 1987

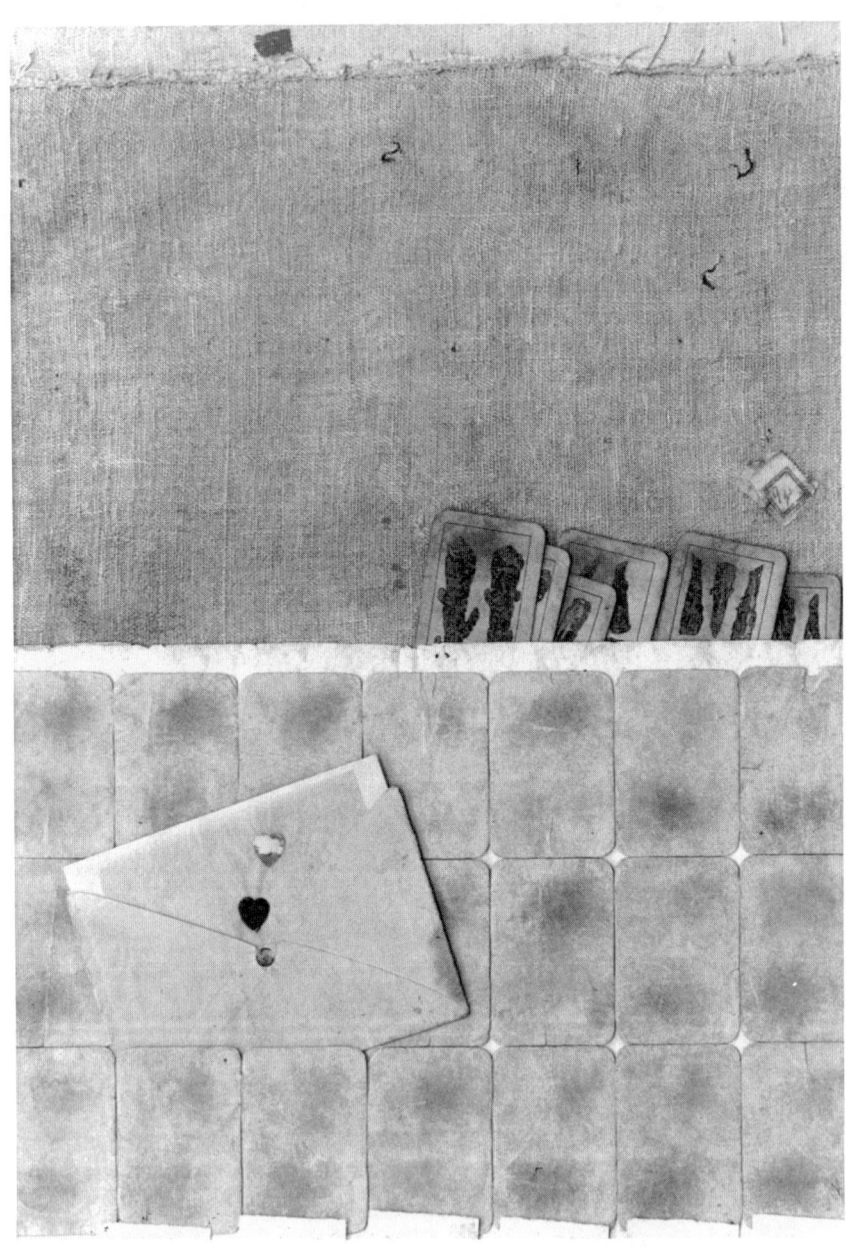

In the Forest (1980). Collage: 21" × 14¾." Judith Young-Mallin collection.

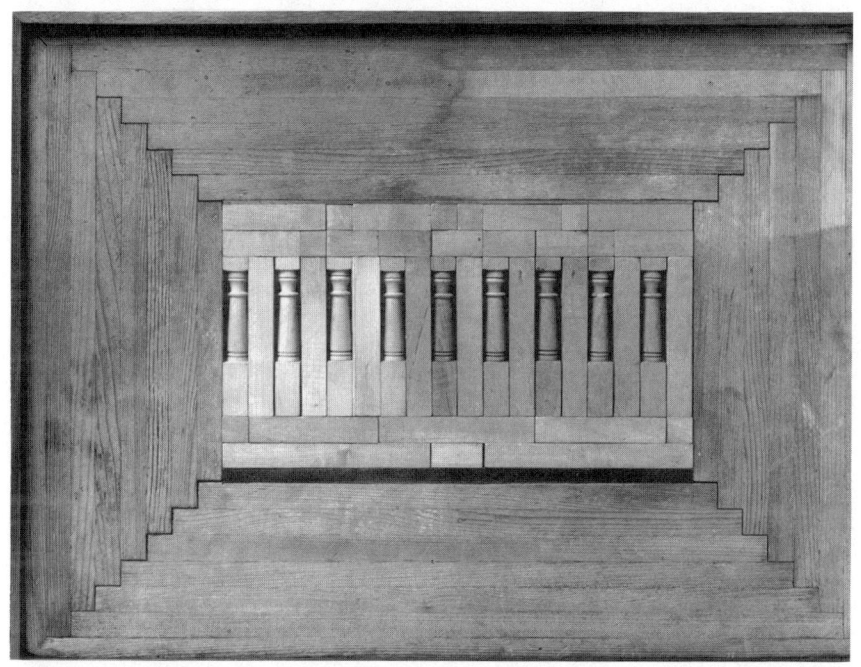

The Temple (1987). Construction: 22″ × 30⅝″ × 2.″ Private collection.

The Fall of Icarus (1986). Construction: 27″ × 19⅝″ × 3.″ Private collection.

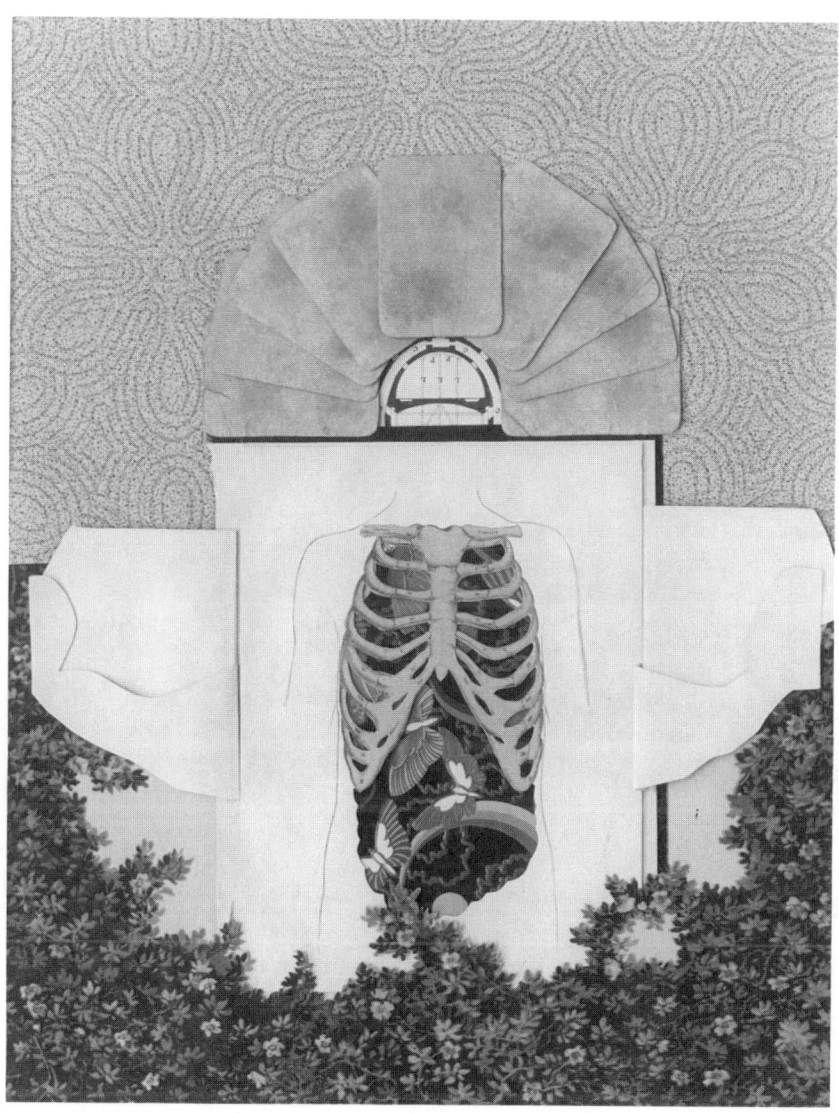

The Cage (1980). Collage: 19" × 15." Private collection.

Orpheus (1983). Construction: 13″ × 17″ × 3½.″ Private collection.

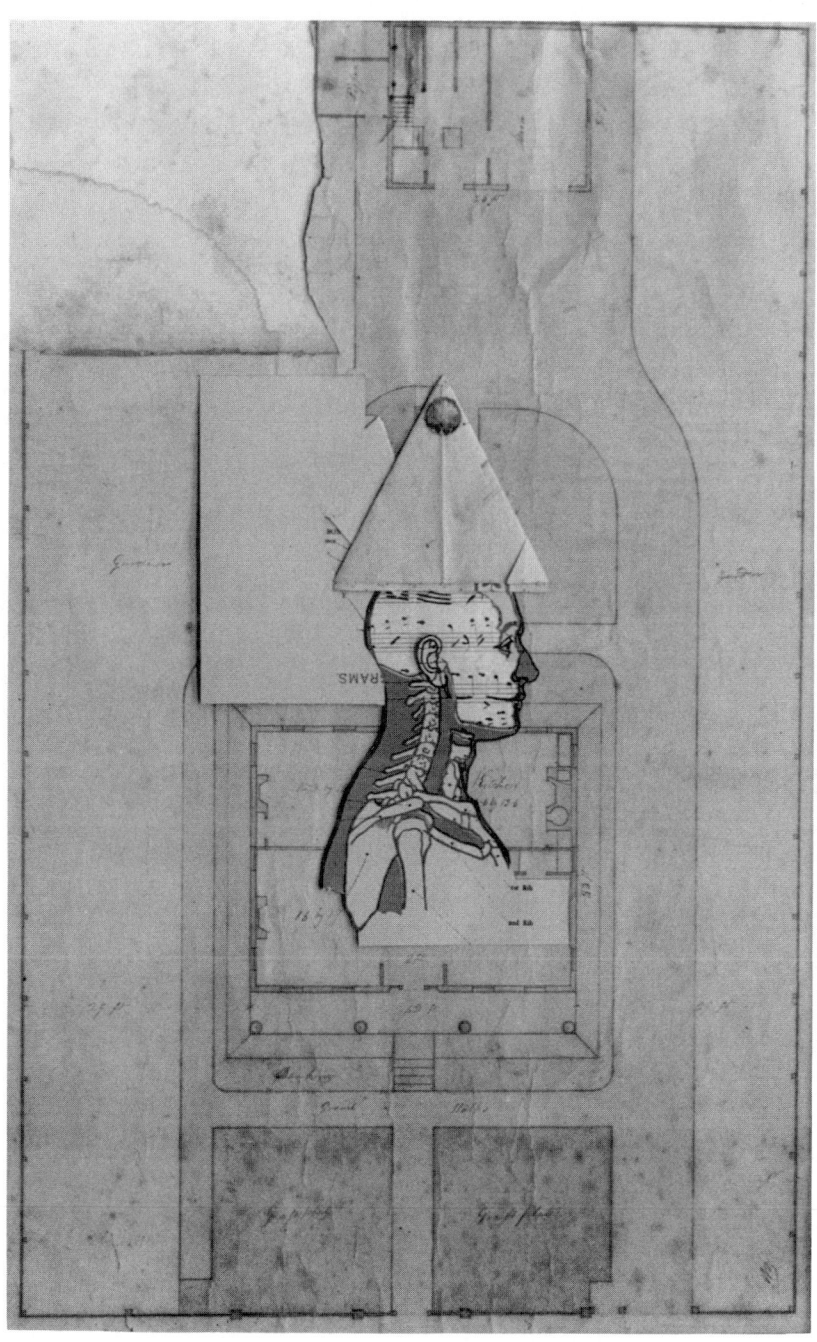

The Musicmaker (1980). Collage: 20½″ × 13.″ Private collection.

Florentine (1987). Construction: 16″ × 17½″ × 1¾.″ Private collection.

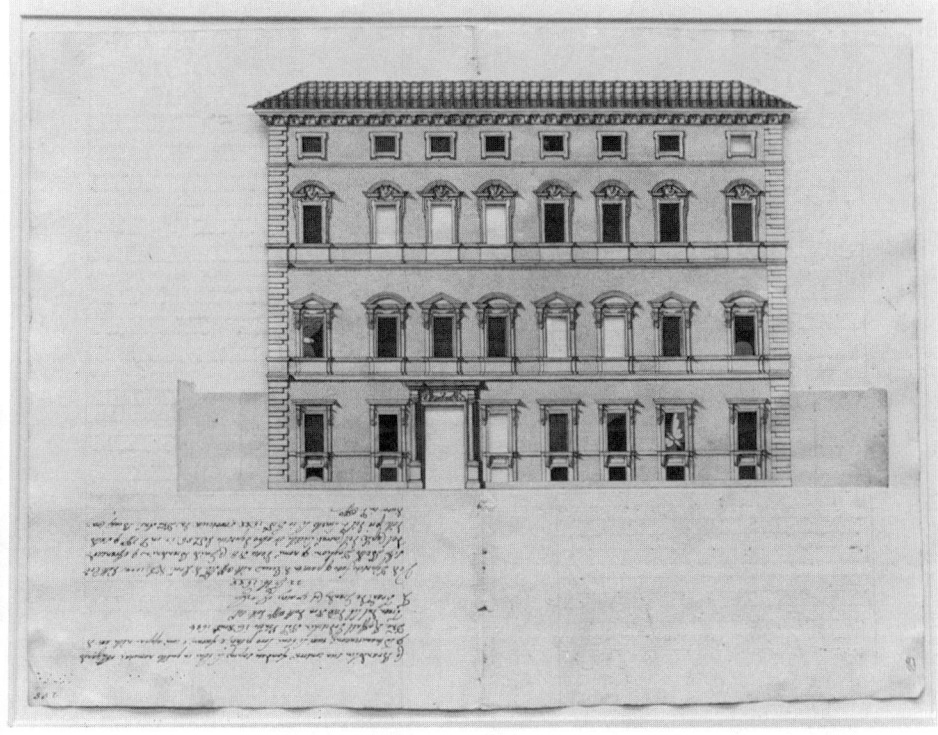

The Fall of Icarus (1980). Collage: 17¼″ × 30.″ Dr. and Mrs. Richard Wolff collection.

The Pierced Heart (1981). Construction: 48" × 22¼" × 17." Sherry Hope Mallin collection.

Chariot (1979). Construction: 28½" × 13½" × 30."

The Magic Mountain (1978). Collage: 8" × 10½." Judith Young-Mallin collection.

Bound Orpheus (1981). Construction: 48" × 22¼" × 17." Sherry Hope Mallin collection.

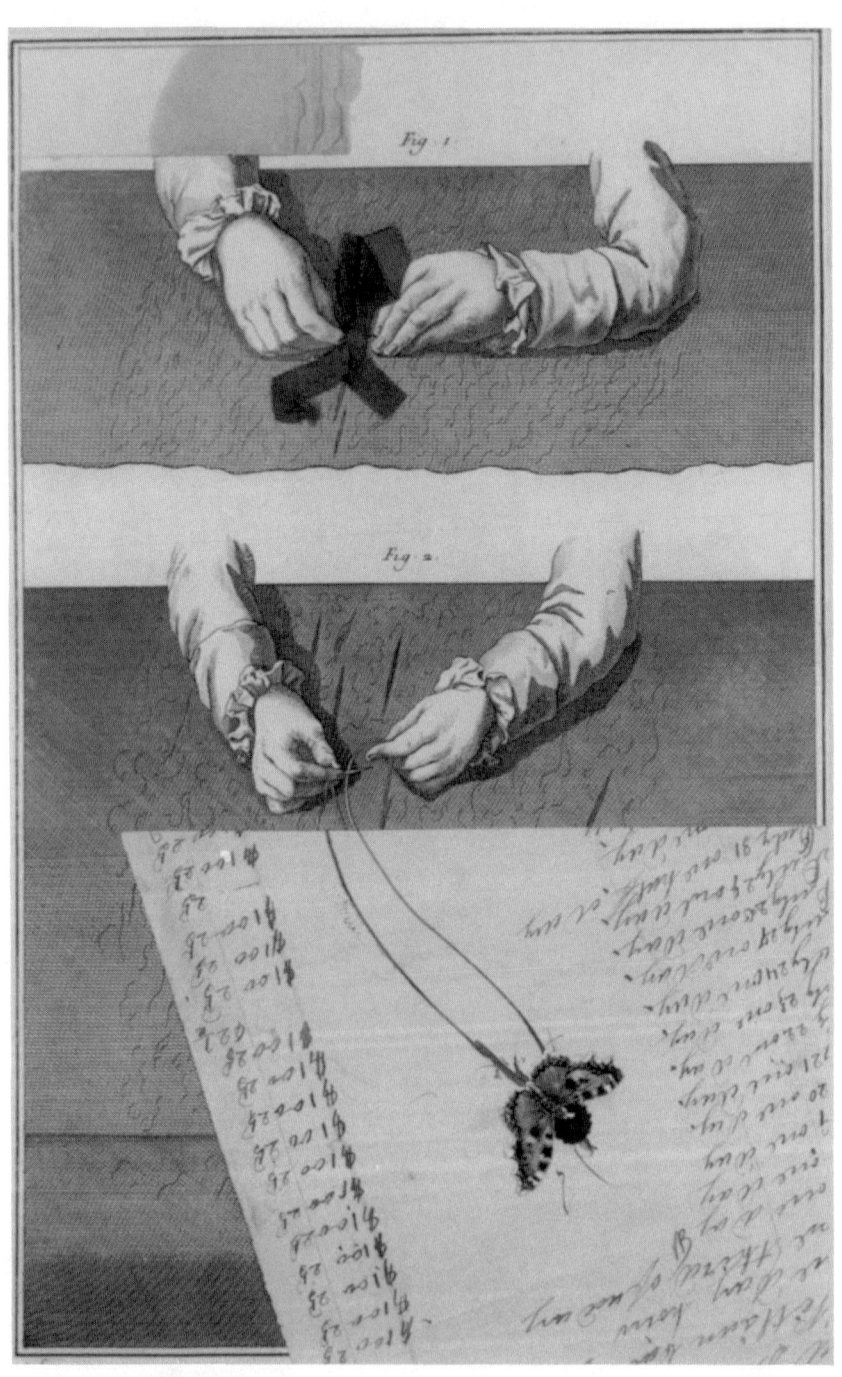

Pluto's Ledger (1980). Collage: 12½″ × 8.″ Private collection.

Facade (1987). Construction: 15⅞" × 11⅛" × 1¾." Private collection.

Grey Day Study (1969). Construction: 36″ × 26¾″ × 4.″ Private collection.

Drowning (1979). Collage: 12″ × 10½.″ Private collection.

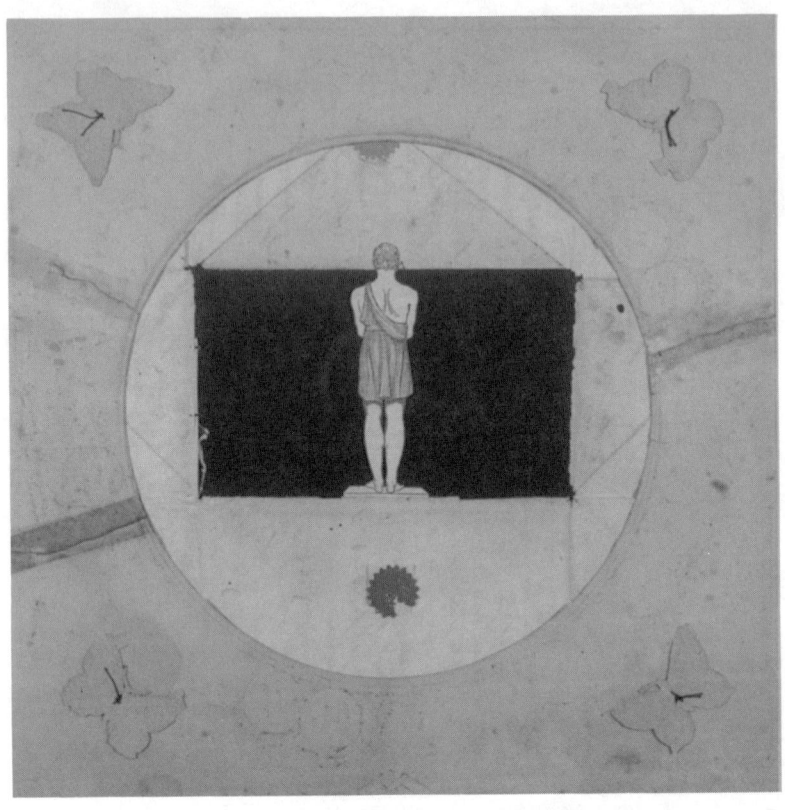

Orpheus (1985). Collage: 10" × 10." Private collection.

Tokens (1977). Construction: 22¾" × 35½" × 3." Private collection.

Feeder (1971). Construction: 60" × 28" × 10." Private collection.

Bells (1980). Construction: 10¾" × 10¾" × 2." Private collection.

Mime (1982). Construction: 32″ × 10″ × 2½.″ Sherry Hope Mallin collection.

The Rose (1980). Collage: 9" × 5½." Private collection.

Crossing the Styx (1965). Construction: 41" × 32½" × 1½."

1
MEANING IN NATIVE AMERICAN ASTRONOMY TEXTS

ANTHONY F. AVENI

Looking into the past, we find cultures very different from our own, yet we find people doing many of the things we do—discovering celestial order through observation, developing calendars, creating cosmologies. As scientists, we often endeavor to explain the unknown by seeking likenesses with known phenomena. However, we must be particularly careful when using this strategy to study the astronomy of other cultures, for we often become enticed into thinking that their motivations and goals were the same as ours. Warning of this "presentist" trap, in the thick of the Stonehenge controversy two decades ago, a historian commented that every age fabricates the Stonehenge it desires. Perhaps we can gain confidence by convincing ourselves that prehistoric Newtons and Einsteins were preaching and practicing our outlook millennia ago. But were they?

An eminent Mayanist once casually dismissed the notion that the ancient inhabitants of Yucatan could have been serious mathematicians and astronomers by suggesting that Maya astronomy was astrology pure and simple. However, in civilizations such as that of the Maya, their world views derived from a close connection between nature and the divine. In these cultures, religion and ritual behavior were not detrimental to the development of astronomy, but were the vital driving force behind it. Moreover, history teaches us that the desire to foretell human affairs motivated those who laid the foundation of our own scientific edifice. Astrology lay behind Kepler's drive to know the precise courses of the planets, and it served also as the principal motivation of the Babylonians—our predecessors in astronomical science.

In ancient civilization there was no apparent bond between

technology and the acquisition of precise knowledge, and our Western notions of scientific progress and man's control over nature appear to have been almost entirely absent. Thus, if we are to gain a clear understanding of the astronomical pursuits of those civilizations, we must be prepared to view their activity through the colored glasses of their cultures.

An excursion through the basics of New World archaeoastronomy, a field that has undergone explosive development this past decade, will show us that in addition to the mere listing of the objects observed and the prevision with which they were reckoned, much is to be learned from examining the astronomies of other cultures. Research in native American astronomy is particularly significant because, until the Spanish conquest, American cultures lay isolated by two oceans from all significant outside influences. Thus, we have a rare chance to learn how people in different times and places developed a knowledge of nature. Understanding this may give us special insight into our own science.

Archaeoastronomy is the study of the indigenous written and unwritten record relating to the practice of astronomy in the ancient world. The breaking of ground in this modern interdisciplinary field began in the early 1960s with astronomer Gerald Hawkins's pioneering work[1] on Stonehenge, which rekindled the idea that the great megalithic edifice was built to serve as a storehouse of alignments to key solar and lunar positions at the horizon. After more than a decade of debate between astronomers and archaeologists over the role of astronomy in the design of ancient ceremonial centers (a confrontation with territorial overtones), there has emerged in the 1980s a spirit of cooperation across the disciplines that has resulted in the formation of a number of research teams to which physical scientists have contributed enormously. The historical branch of the American Astronomical Society now lists papers on archeoastronomy at the society's national meetings, and in the past two years physicists and astronomers have contributed to three international meetings on the subject.

A developed system of astronomy can be characterized by the systematic gathering, classification, and storage of precise astronomical data accompanied by the creation and refinement of a methodology for reaching important future dates—what we would call a calendar. We expect to find such astronomy among high civilizations, which need uniform time systems to delineate formally the timing of festivals, planting, and the payment of tributes. The time base maintained by a developed state allows the collection of astronomical observations and the recognition of the periodicities necessary for setting up a calendar. Moreover, an organized society usually develops a means of transmitting acquired knowledge about the heavens, often through a written record. This tells us where to look to find developed astronomies in the Americas: among those civilizations that by all definitive standards achieved a high state of development—the Mayas and Aztecs of Mexico, and perhaps the Incas of Peru.

Pre-Columbian astronomies flourished in South America, Central America, Mexico, and North America. Since it is not possible to cover all of their activity in detail, we will devote much of our discussion to one example, the Maya of Mexico, a group whose astronomical activity is rather well documented. First, we will look at the Maya written record, which includes a very accurate Venus ephemeris. Then we will survey the architectural record—the astronomical alignments of surviving structures. We will proceed to take a brief look at North American Indian astronomy, on which much research remains to be done. Finally, we will discuss some implications of the growing recognition that the key to understanding an astronomy is understanding the cultural context in which it is practiced.

Perhaps what excites us most about the ancient Maya of Mesoamerica (the latitudes of eastern Mexico that include the Yucatan) is that in addition to creating monumental architecture and exquisite sculpture and painting, they also had developed a system of writing and numeration. When we examine the handful of books that survived the Spanish conquest and the scores of carved monuments that the Maya once displayed publicly in ceremonial centers such as Tikal and Palenque, we discover a grammar like our own and a syllabary composed of more than eight hundred hieroglyphs. Some of these symbols represent astronomical objects and concepts.

Epigraphic studies shortly after the turn of the century[2] revealed that the Maya had a numeration system with place-value notation and a concept of zero. Though we might be frightened away by the grotesque-looking pictorial accompaniments to the dot-bar numerals and hieroglyphs that appear in depictions of Maya calendars, a penetrating look at one of its pages reveals that, like most Maya documents, astronomy bares its presence behind the veil of ritual. Adjacent to the Venus table in the Dresden Codex, or manuscript, named after the city in whose library it turned up three centuries after the conquest, is a tabulation that gives the dates of past solar and lunar eclipses as well as a means for predicting future eclipses.

The Maya achieved the eclipse algorithm by grouping lunar phase counts in clusters of 6 and 5, defined canonically as 177- and 148-day periods. Apparently they realized from long experience that it was only after certain combinations of such period-clusters that visible eclipses did indeed occur. The Maya mapped out the entire eclipse program for the future with neither knowledge of nor interest in the concept of the nodes of the lunar orbit or the nineteen-year nodal regression period that has been given so much attention in megalithic astronomy of the Old World, where it is said to have been detected in the horizon extremes of the rising and setting moon.[3] Instead, Maya astronomy gives the appearance of an almost purely temporal affair that made no use of orbits, heliocentrism, or geocentrism—or indeed any centrism. Both the eclipse and Venus tables in the Dresden Codex contain only numbers and cycles that churn together like so many interlocking odometers to give forth predictions.

A closer look at the Dresden ephemeris may help clarify the Maya astronomical system. The table, which is recyclable, is 37,960 days long (about 104 years), a number the Maya undoubtedly chose because it is a multiple of the 584-day interval between successive conjunctions of Venus and the Sun, a 260-day Mayan ritual count generated by matching 13 numbers with 20 named days, and the 365-day approximation to the tropical year. The Maya were especially aware of the 8:5 ratio between the lengths of the Venus and Earth years, a discovery revealed to them through observation of the eight-year seasonal recurrence of Venus phenomena. Our way of classifying the planets heliocentrically might lead us to lose sight of the special relationship in the sky between the Sun and Venus that the Maya seem to have emphasized. Unlike all the other planets (save Mercury), Venus follows closely upon the course of the Sun, never deviating by more than 46 degrees from the Sun's position. Thus, the planet appears as the evening star in the west after which it is blocked by the Sun. During this period of blockage, known to us as inferior conjunction, Venus passes in front of the Sun. Following this, one views Venus as the morning star in the east, only later to find it disappearing into the Sun once again by passing behind it.

The planet's predawn heliacal rise, or first appearance after invisibility due to conjunction with the Sun, is symbolized by the appearance in the North of Kukulcán, the god of Venus. Like the visible aspects of Venus, Kukulcán symbolizes the cyclic myth of departure and return (or death and resurrection) in the Maya world view. Indeed, in central Mexico the Aztecs confused Cortez with the returning Quetzalcoatl, their version of Kukulcán, whose return they anticipated precisely at the time of the Spanish invasion. Kukulcán appears in the middle panel of each page of the Venus table flinging spears of dazzling rays of light— evil omens—at victims depicted in the lower panels. The rays represent the incipient light of the resurrected god who had previously absented himself from view. The reappearance of Venus in different quarters after a prolonged absence evidently carried various evil connotations for the people of Yucatan.

At the bottom of each page of the table we find Venus's 584-day year or synodic cycle broken down, not into the periods we would expect from reading one of our own astronomy texts, but rather into periods corresponding to the planet's four celestial stations described above. Venus is said to spend its 584 days as follows, with the actual mean periods given in parentheses: 236 days as the morning star (263 days); 90 days in the disappearance interval around superior conjunction (50 days); 250 days as the evening star (263 days); 8 days in the disappearance interval around inferior conjunction (8 days). It is after the critical 8-day disappearance of Venus that the Venus god Kukulcán rises heliacally and flings his spears of light, thus casting evil upon Earth.

At first glance these erroneous numbers might lead us to to conclude that the Maya were totally incapable of pinning down the great luminary. How else could they misclock one of the disappearance intervals by more than a month? But looking more closely at the calendar we discover that, like so many other numbers that appear in the Maya inscriptions, these intervals are contrived to blend with other numbers. For example, there are 236 days in 8 lunar months.

Whether this fact reveals a Maya attempt to relate Venus and lunar cycles in concrete observational terms, scholars cannot say at this stage. However, it seems very likely that one motive behind the selection of these deceptive looking numbers lay in a ritual constraint that was built into the calendar. The Maya believed that only certain of the twenty named days that repeat to make up the 260-day cycle could be used to celebrate the transition of the planet from one celestial station to the next. This notion parallels our habit of insisting that Washington's birthday be celebrated on a Monday even if that day is not the real anniversary of the event.

Examining these named days, which appear written across the table in 13 horizontal lines at the top of each page, historian of science Sharon Gibbs has argued that the canonic intervals probably were chosen to guarantee celebration of the Venus appearance closest to but not before the planet's actual first appearance. In fact, she showed that the tabulated intervals link specifically designated ritual dates occurring as close as possible to the events of last and first visibility without actually ever occurring during disappearance.[4] Indeed, such a ritual constraint would have placed a taxing burden upon the astronomer, for not only would he have to observe and record celestial events, but he would also have to worry about displaying his data in such a fashion that it exhibits certain commensurabilities with respect to nonastronomical cycles emanating from another quarter.

Paradoxically, even though Maya chronologists seem to be bowing to ritual by falsifying short-term Venus events, current research indicates that by the middle of the tenth century they had developed a correction scheme to keep Venus's canonic 584-day cycle of events on track with its true synodic period of 483.92 days. Expressed in our terms, the scheme, which called for the periodic omission of certain segments of the count, was accurate to the day over half a millennium. Such accuracy exceeds all attempts up to the Gregorian reform of our own calendar to keep an accurate account of the annual solar cycle.

Given such a precise calendar, we wonder: What observations are necessary to predict the heliacal rise of Venus, and is there any evidence in the surviving record about the modus operandi of Maya astronomy? Unlike the Babylonians, the Maya appear to have left us no observing logs or "notebooks" delineating a record of their sightings. The codices seem to represent only the finished product—the public side of their science.

An important clue lay hidden for a long time in the standing architecture. The last decade of Maya research has shown that many structures are aligned toward astronomical events occurring at the horizon. A Spanish historian tells us quite specifically that in ancient Mexico City, King Montezuma wished to arrange his principal Aztec temple so that the Sun would rise over the middle of it at the equinoxes, and that when the architects failed in their first attempt, they were forced to tear it down and straighten it! Such an act should come as no surprise once we understand Aztec and Maya ceremonial centers as places for the performance of important rituals. Moreover, it is reasonable to anticipate an emphasis on horizon alignments in the astronomies of people living in tropical latitudes. In the higher latitudes, diurnal motion clearly involves circulation about a pole. Celestial objects near the horizon move sideways as well as up and down as they rise or set. However, in tropical skies stars rise and set along tracks that are nearly vertical with respect to the horizon, making it easy for equatorial observers to classify directions on Earth by celestial reference points.

The precise time and place of the last visibility of Venus at the western horizon (before the planet moves in front of the Sun) constitutes an index of the length of time that the planet will remain obscured by the Sun during inferior conjunction.[5] Therefore, we might expect that any Venus watcher in the tropics would set up horizon alignments to the West. Also, we might anticipate observation of the planet's horizon standstill positions. We find that while these horizon extremes occur on an annual basis as Venus moves more or less with the Sun, a seasonal cycle of great extremes repeats almost exactly after an eight-year interval, which is a period given considerable attention in the Dresden Codex.

At Chichén Itzá, the Maya, after their tenth-century A.D. conquest by the Toltecs, preserved precisely these Venus orientations in the Caracol, a round observatory building located at the ruins of Chichén Itzá, Yucatán, Mexico. The Caracol was erected about the same time the Dresden Codex was written, and is said to have been dedicated to the Venus god Kukulcán. Using surveyor's transit and astronomical fix, architect Horst Hartung, Sharon Gibbs, and I found that a pair of diagonals in the windows of the turret, and another pair of alignments in the base of the building, point to within ½ degree on the average of the places where Venus set over the Western horizon at southerly and northerly standstills around 1000 A.D., when archaeologists tell us the building was completed. More importantly, the origin of the Dresden Codex can be placed both in space and time quite close to Chichén Itzá. Thus, it is not too large a leap to suggest that the Caracol was the very astronomical observatory that lay behind the written Venus calendar.

Other buildings in Yucatán aligned to Venus include the palace of the governor at Uxmal. Its long façade and principal doorway face 28 degrees 05 minutes south of east, which is within two minutes of arc of the southerly standstill position of Venus in 750 A.D., when the palace is thought to have been built. Moreover, the entire structure, which was built on an artificial mound 400 meters on a side, is misaligned by 20 degrees with respect to the other buildings at Uxmal, thus emphasizing its special nature and lending some force to the astronomical hypothesis. The principal pyramid at the ruins of Cehtzuc is the only visible feature from the governor's doorway on an otherwise flat horizon. It bears 28 degrees 13 minutes south of east at a range of 6 km, or just 15 m off the perpendicular. Moreover, this pyramid accurately marked the "turn-around" point in the eight-year Venus cycle, which occurred at 28 degrees 03 minutes south of east.

Just as archaeological data reinforced the hypotheses of astronomical orientation both at Chichén Itzá and Uxmal, so, too, iconographic evidence comes to the aid of astronomy at the governor's palace. Close inspection reveals that the cornice of the building is adorned with over three hundred Venus glyphs carved in stone—the same ones that appear in the Venus table of the Codex. Also, the figure of a Maya rain god that appears at the northeast cornerstone of the building displays on its forehead the number eight—three dots suspended from a bar—which may signify Venus's eight-day disappearance before heliacal rise, or perhaps its eight-year cycle.

The use of the surveyor's transit to collect data on the astronomical orientation of sites in Central Mexico has revealed the interesting fact that all the sites are skewed clockwise from the north (looking down from above). This habit probably arose from a tradition established at Teotihuacán, the most expansive and influential site in all of Mexico, which flourished about the time of the beginning of the Christian era. Examples of Teotihuacán forms of pottery and architecture are found all over Mexico and Central America, including Maya Yucatán. At Teotihuacán, located near Mexico City, we find both a cardinal grid plan, that is, a grid oriented north-south and east-west, and a plan skewed to align with horizon events that may involve the Pleiades, a group of stars of central importance in Mesoamerican star lore. An equinox alignment discovered in the fifteenth-century Aztec ruins of Tenochtitlán also has been documented at Teotihuacán fifteen hundred years earlier, thus suggesting a long astronomical tradition.

At the ruins of Alta Vista (near Chalchihuites, Mexico) we find evidence that colonists from Teotihuacán had attempted to find where on Earth the Sun turned around, that is, the tropic, where the Sun rises to the zenith at noon only for a day, and then returns to the south of the zenith for all other days of the year. We have come to identify the day as the June solstice. At Alta Vista, which is very near the tropic of Cancer, and at Teotihuacán, we find identical petroglyphs carved in stone and in the floors of buildings to mark significant alignments. These symbols, of which more than fifty are known throughout Mexico, usually appear as a double circle centered on a cross. The curious design is made up of holes hammered into stucco or rock with a percussive device.

These discoveries may indicate a widespread organized attempt to institute calendric principles on a "nationwide" basis. However, we sense that at least among the Maya, astronomy still was governed by a ritual elite whose secret methods and knowledge were not shared with the man in the field. We can only wonder whether an esotericism of advanced astronomy and a consequent detachment between rulers and people might have contributed to the precipitous collapse of the Maya civilization on the eve of the Spanish conquest of the Americas.

We have tried to suggest that the sky presents all of humankind with a set of universals; everywhere the Sun rises and sets, attains its horizon extremes, and participates in eclipses. Thus, the sky becomes a laboratory for testing the question: Do all cultures react in the same way to the phenomena that pass before our eyes? However, interpreting reactions is not simple, and archaeoastronomers confront a problem that faces all students of antiquity: Have we exaggerated the degree to which ancient people thought like us? We can avoid the pitfall of creating false images of ourselves in the past only by gaining a broad knowledge of the people whose astronomy we study. We must know about their religion and ritual, their art and sculpture, even the organization of their families. For the researcher trained in the physical sciences, a serious venture into archaeoastronomy requires a substantial commitment, but the experience of learning about another culture's view of nature can be very rewarding.

With a growing recognition that the cultural context holds the key to understanding ancient astronomy, New World archaeoastronomy has begun to flourish as evidence from ethnology, epigraphy, archaeology, and mythology has joined the alignment data. One lesson we learn from the interdisciplinary study is that things often turn out to be different from what we might have anticipated. For example, the rebuilt Aztec structure at Tenochtitlán to which we referred earlier is oriented precisely to the equinox sunrise even though it is misaligned with the east-west line by 7 degrees. Only the written evidence tells us that the skew was due to the fact that the observation was made over an elevated surface, so that the Sun was observed only after it had moved some distance along the slanted path on which it rises. This example illustrates how far we may be from arriving at the truth if we follow the simple research path that isolates astronomy from the context in which it actually was practiced.

Finally, we will all wonder: Is it correct to call the practice of the ancients scientific astronomy? Asger Aaboe,[6] a historian of Old World science, gives us one of the most explicit definitions of scientific astronomy. He defines an astronomical theory to be scientific only when it "gives us control over the irregularities within each [astronomical] period and thus frees us from constant consultation of observation records." Such a theory is, essentially, "a mathematical description of celestial phenomena capable of yielding numerical predictions that can be tested against observations." Aaboe uses as examples Babylonian lunar texts from the Seleucid Era. It can be shown that the precise positions of solar and lunar conjunctions given in these texts could not have come from direct observations but rather must have derived from the application of certain purely mathematical functions that Babylonian astronomers had developed. Aaboe distinguishes scientific astronomy from the less advanced primitive astronomy, which is a kind of passive pastoral activity of recognizing constellations and marking the appearance and disappearance intervals of planets as evening or morning stars—the sort of celestial behavior to which one assigns certain "rustic tasks."

This definition, should we press it, can be fulfilled to varying degrees by the cultures we have examined. The Maya, with their precise Venus warning table, would score high; the Chumash of California, perhaps somewhat lower. But what does it mean to ask of every astronomical pursuit—is it science? One can argue that Aaboe's definition is culture-laden, specifically, that his standard of science is the result of over three thousand years of evolution along a particular path, during which elements of culture that affect our definition of science have changed. That evolutionary process included the rise of the Greek ideal and the industrial revolution, to mention but two important developments that influenced the course of western science. Have we any reason to expect other people to think as we do if they did not evolve along the same cultural lines? From this point of view, to ask "is it science?" is almost to ask if it is the product of Western culture.

There is abundant literature on the contrasts between traditional modes of thought and Western science; the differences appear to be vast. For example, as Cornell anthropologist Billie

Jean Isbell has suggested,[7] the system of classification that underlies Western science seeks similarities against backgrounds of differences. On the other hand, Native American thought systems seem to be organized around a dialectic that stresses simultaneous interdependence and contradiction. Applied to astronomy, this principle argues that, for example, Andean astronomical phenomena are perceived only as dual pairs, such as the zenith sunrise and antizenith sunset alignments, which were prominent in the structure of Cuzco, capital of the Inca empire.

An awareness of the vast differences between Western and traditional modes of thought will lead us to ask different questions. Among some indigenous people of South America, a woodpecker's beak applied to an aching tooth is said to provide the cure. We might ask: How can a bird beak effect a cure? However, as anthropologist Claude Levi-Strauss commented:

> The real question is not whether the touch of a woodpecker's beak does in fact cure toothache. It is rather whether there is a point of view from which a woodpecker's beak and a man's tooth can be seen as "going together" (the use of this congruity for therapeutic purposes being only one of its possible uses), and whether some initial order can be introduced into the universe by means of these groupings.[8]

Perhaps we are fully beginning to ask a few correct questions about Native American astronomies.

Notes

1. G. Hawkins and J. White, *Stonehenge Decoded* (New York: Delta Dell, 1965).
2. S. G. Morley, *An Introduction to the Study of the Maya Hieroglyphs*, Bur. Am. Ethnol. (Smithsonian Inst.), no. 57 (1915); J. Teeple, *Maya Astronomy* (Washington, D.C.: Carn. Inst. Wash., 1930).
3. A. Thom, *Megalithic Lunar Observatories* (London: Oxford University Press, 1971).
4. S. Gibbs, "Mesoamerican Calendrics as evidence of astronomical activity," in *Native American Astronomy*, ed. A. F. Aveni (Austin: University of Texas Press, 1977), pp. 21–35.
5. A. F. Aveni, *Skywatchers of Ancient Mexico* (Austin: University of Texas Press, 1980).

6. A. Aaboe, Phil. "Scientific Astronomy in Antiquity," *Philosophical Transactions of the Royal Society* (London)

7. B. J. Isbell, "Culture Confronts Nature in the Dialectical World of the Tropics," in *Archaeoastronomy & Ethnoastronomy in the American Tropics*, ed. A. F. Aveni and G. Urton (New York: New York Academy of Science, 1982), pp. 353–63.

8. C. Lévi-Strauss, *The Raw and the Cooked* (New York: Harper & Row, 1969).

2

BOGHOSIAN ON BOGHOSIAN

VARUJAN BOGHOSIAN

The topic, *Transforming Texts,* is indicative of what I have been doing since I began to work as an artist. In the process, I have also been transformed. Many of my constructions deal with a visualization of music and love. Symbolic of these themes is the image of the heart with bells around the edges of a bread board, recalling visually the wonderful sound they give out. Many of the objects and images from my boyhood were recalled in these works. A wonderful auditory image, which has stayed with me since childhood, is the sound of the rag man as he rode down the street in his horse-drawn cart calling, "rags, purrags, rags, purrags!" Years later, I realized that I was using rags in my work, along with small nails. My father was a cobbler who would repair our shoes at night, and I still remember the image of him with a mouth full of nails, pounding them into leather soles. I also used hat block forms and transformed them into the images of Pluto. I found myself pounding little nails into the hat block forms, and it brought back the memories of my father. Transformation takes place in so many ways: transferring, transforming, transporting.

The origins of my work began with my love of poetry. When I came out of the service in World War II, I attended a teachers' college under the G.I. Bill and my fondest dream was to be a poet. Fortunately I had a wonderful teacher, Constance Carrier, who was a poet; we would meet after school in a little diner and talk about poetry. My poetry had to do with life, death, and all of those wonderful big topics, and somehow or other she steered me into the Orpheus myth. She told me about Orpheus, Eurydice, Pluto, and my first endeavor was to do a series of woodcuts. After that I wrote poems which illustrated the various steps or stages in the myth of Orpheus. Not being a scholar in this area, I looked at the myth very simply. I worked with the raw basic myth and then made elaborations on it in the constructions. The meaning of the myth for me is in the three principal characters: the hero Orpheus, Eurydice, and Pluto. These three characters formed a triangle which was very complex and yet also quite simple. The agonies which confronted Orpheus in his loss of Eurydice are comparable to the problems that Pluto faced. Pluto's similar dilemma involved having his wife, Persephone, spend half of the year in the underworld and then releasing her to the earth. Thus Orpheus's great sorrow in losing Eurydice was an emotion he had in common with Pluto. His journey to Hades was an expression of this sorrow as well as an attempt to resolve the problem. The sadness which results from human loss is a pervasive, universal emotion, and is common to all people.

The basic elements of the Orpheus myth have consistently appeared in my constructions over the years: the key figure or hero, the boat, symbolic of the journey, and the heart, which represents love and/or the sense of loss. It has not been difficult to stay with the Orpheus myth for this length of time because all of the various details and levels of interpretation mean very little to me in and of themselves. For instance, I am not concerned with the interrelationships between Hermes, Apollo, and Orpheus, or what they signified to one another. I very simply have characters to work with, and I change them in all sorts of ways, while paring down the myth to its essentials. In the earlier work the ornamentation and elaboration of each element within the construction was more extensive, but I began to realize that this elaboration had nothing to do with the basic myth except as filler to bolster the composition. I have been attempting to get away from that embellishing tendency so as to get down to the crux of the matter.

My first visualizations of the myth were woodcuts, and when I finished this series, I began to search for three-dimensional material with which to work. Many of these forms and shapes were found by accident, but others were located or sent by friends and colleagues. I began to frequent antique shops and flea markets and thus began a strange quest similar to that of Orpheus; the difference being that he was searching for someone and I was searching for something.

My studio in Hanover, New Hampshire, contains a thirty-year

collection of objects of all manner, shape, size, and color to use in the myth. It is necessary to have a great number and variety of pieces from which to choose if one is to be a successful constructionist or collage maker. It cannot be done with seven Civil War photographs, two small boxes, a child's top, and a few rags. This is especially true when one is dealing with a complex myth with many aspects to it. The real difficulty is in the finding of the various material. One must have more than enough in order to make that unbelievable marriage or magic fit that brings the myth to life. Over the years I have used hundreds of fragments, yet most of the material in my studio has yet to be transformed into finished constructions. This stockpile of material is what compels me to keep working. When I am in the studio, surrounded with so many objects, I feel like a businessman who has a terrific investment in stock which must be put to use. There are times, of course, when I do get tired of looking at so many things collected over the years. Occasionally I walk into the studio and look at my collection and then just turn around and walk out. I am still, however, terrifically motivated and excited by the limitless potential of all that I possess.

The search for materials is an endless one and requires a great deal of patience. Often I find that I need an additional element in order to finish a given work, or possibly a third or fourth element to complete it. For instance, one unfinished construction in my studio consists of a glass heart, broken in half, resting on another old piece of glass. Visitors to the studio have asked me when I will finish it. The construction has been there for three years, unfinished, because I have not been able to find the final element. A missing piece is often found by accident, although, if I keep my eyes attuned, I most often find what I am looking for. A typical experience for me is when I have spotted an expensive game board at a large antique show—and then proceeded to walk around the entire floor, looking for another object to fit with the board. Although it seldom works out that I discover two or more elements this way, when it does happen it means that I have planned a construction right there on that spot. At any given time, I might have half a dozen or more uncompleted constructions that have been in the studio for three or four years awaiting completion. In looking for materials, I am intuitively drawn to that which is old. New material does not, as a rule, hold any appeal for me because it lacks the time-worn color and texture that I feel comfortable with. Occasionally the material is relatively recent, such as thirty-year-old playing cards which were staining and wearing brought about from constant use. There have been times when I have used new material, but I have found that it was unsatisfactory because it lacked the endless, timeless quality that I am always looking for. If a paper material from the last thirty years is mellowed with bent edges, damaged from the use of a child's hand or from a dog that chewed on it, I will find a use for it.

I will often alter that material to the specifications and mood of the myth. For instance, the small figure blowing a trumpet in Pluto's temple looks timeless, yet when I found the figure, it was one of twenty World War I soldiers blowing the bugle in a khaki military uniform. In order to use the figure in the context of the myth, I gently sanded away the aspect of the uniform, and then, with fine steel wool, brushed it down to anonymous lead. Two of these same figures were used again in *Crossing the River Styx*, in which two anonymous musicians are blowing trumpets as they make their way across the river. Destruction is sometimes necessary to create something new. In other instances, I have used the head of Napoleon, with a bit of camouflage, to signify the head of Orpheus, although the two were separated by many centuries. This was possible because Napoleon had a very classical and simple-featured face.

The letters which I use in my collages are usually very old, and although I love them, I am not concerned with their content. More often than not, they are placed upside down in the composition so that the actual message on the letter does not interfere with the meaning of the work. What is important for me is that the letters' colors, markings, and linear aspects serve as either foreground or background devices in relation to the key image of the work. These letters, which are usually found in flea markets, become like drawings, and in the case of the collage of Eurydice, they represent the menacing maze of her situation, and of her looking backward.

A central motif in the Orpheus myth is the love which existed between Orpheus and Eurydice. Intertwined with the love theme is the idea of music. Orpheus was so endowed with the great ability to sing and play that everything else was transformed and enchanted by his music, which is represented by birds, bells, sheet music, and other musical instruments. The images of the heart symbolizes the love aspect of the myth as well as the sense of loss. I have dealt with the tortured idea of the heart in agony or distress by using a very old, heart-shaped pincushion studded with rusty little pins and a single pearl. In a departure from the Orpheus myth, I used the pearl in a work based on Nathaniel Hawthorne's *The Scarlet Letter* to represent Hester Prynne's love child who was named Pearl.

There are certain objects that I have found could be used over and over again because they served the myth so well, such as the mannequin. Along the way I have been fortunate to find many slat-figured mannequins in all sizes. Most of them were found in Italy, but occasionally, I have found them in New York antique shops. Another object that I have frequently used, particularly in the beginning, is the wooden ironing board. I felt that, like a wonderful canvas, this was a terrific shape. When I first found these ironing boards in junk shops or at the Salvation Army, I would tear the cloth off the board so as to get at the wood underneath. However, I soon began to realize that the cloth itself had a wonderful quality to it—certain stains where the iron may have been forgotten for a brief period of time or patches of sheeting which had been put on while still leaving the old cloth underneath. As I began to tear the sheeting away from the board, I suddenly realized the tortured quality of the cloth and decided to leave some of the shreds of the material rather than stripping it right down to the wood as I had done before. The shreds of tattered cloth on the ironing board contributed to the sense of agony in the myth. Along with the ironing board, the early child's slate has a marvelous quality to it and is a material that appears in and out of various compositions that I do. Similarly, children's anchor blocks from the late nineteenth and early twentieth centuries have proven to be effective objects that I have repeatedly used. I continue to find them in sets of red, white, and blue, but they are now getting quite scarce.

The depiction of Orpheus in my work has been predicated by his mythical functions and attributes. In one collage, for instance, the water stains on the pages of an old gold leaf photographic album have a connotative significance. Simple line drawing pages from old student anatomy books have been used in other collages to represent Orpheus. These pages have been juxtaposed with sheets of old paper, such as handwritten music or personal letters. The high pointed hat, used in both the collages and constructions, conveys the aspect of the clown or entertainer. Orpheus as an entertainer, or more specifically as a juggler, is represented by many spherical shapes, such as wooden croquet balls or a multitude of atoms in space.

Although the hat block form with nails was often used, as we shall see, to represent Pluto, it was also used to symbolize Orpheus. I sometimes used the hat block form from the twenties and thirties which functioned to make beautiful ladies' hats and which come apart. These were used in combination with anchor blocks, various pieces of fabric, and such objects as an old shingle maker's bench, a fragment of stained glass, or a lobster buoy. The lobster buoy was used in one piece with a metallic head and both were magnetized so that they could move and become interchangeable. Old manila envelopes have been used repetitiously like waves in the ocean, together with the drowning head of Orpheus.

Several portraits that I have done of Orpheus have been altered over the years. A construction entitled *Rainbow* showed the hero as a head beneath a great metal arc with spokes radiating from it. This work remained in my studio for a number of years until I had the realization that I could put the material to better use in a different structure, in which the central elements no longer existed in their initial form. The construction *Feeder* originally contained a bronze bird, but I needed this element, which refers to Orpheus feeding and in turn being fed, in order to complete another work. In this instance, I intend to replace the bird to restore the work to its original concept.

The part of the myth in which Orpheus embarks on his search for Eurydice in Hades is filled with yearning and desire and is symbolized by stars, shrouds, a hand caught in a goldsmith's vice, and of course, the heart. Several works contain maple syrup molds in the shape of a heart, and occasionally these are embellished with a few tassels and beads. In the course of his journey to Hades, Orpheus must cross the River Styx. The gatekeeper Charon and watch dog Cerberus must be given the coin for passage. This is represented by a heart containing old subway tokens. I have used anchor blocks to depict the river itself with wooden blocks signifying plans on either side, reminiscent of Brancusi's *Endless Column*.

I have used miniature boats in many works to represent the crossing of the River Styx. In one construction, I positioned the boat in the drawer of a cash register, as it holds money for passage across the river. Orpheus's journey takes him to Hades, and I have depicted the underworld in various ways: a spiral, the base of a large column, and the façade of an Italian villa. The villa represents Hades as a container for characters, colors, and shapes. I have used marbleized paper as a background, symbolizing water and turmoil.

Pluto in the underworld was often represented as a wooden hat block with steel nails pounded into the form, which was contained in a wooden packing box. The image of the huge head, which is confined in the too small box, conveys an ominous, foreboding mood. These hat block forms with nails have their origin in my childhood experiences of my father's cobbler shop. In many of these constructions, Orpheus appears as a small figure confronting Pluto, blowing his trumpet and playing his music in an attempt to convince Pluto to release Eurydice.

Eurydice has often been represented by a wooden mannequin, but some of these constructions have been dismantled. One that no longer exists depicted Eurydice as a mannequin in a wooden bathtub. The play of contrasting brown colors of the wood was achieved by taking the copper lining out of the tub so that the wood of the tub and the mannequin flowed together. Eurydice has also been positioned in front of an ironing board, a slate, or an early American ledger. She is often placed in a forest setting and occasionally shown being menaced by a serpent. In many of the constructions and collages, Eurydice is depicted at that decisive moment in the myth where she is looking backward, in a reaction to Orpheus looking back at her.

Orpheus and Eurydice have been presented in combination in many of my works, very often utilizing the various colors of nineteenth-century children's anchor blocks. They have been depicted in this manner as trees, birds, and as night and day. The anchor blocks have enabled me to present various aspects of the two characters in geometric form.

I have done a number of works which fall outside of the Orpheus myth. Certain forms and image I have encountered have moved me in a singular way, and they have become something else. I love the imagery of René Magritte, and I have done a number of homages to him. One construction consisted of a little black derby hat floating above a small house and a butterfly, all contained in a glass box. The house is a wonderful little middle-class house that Magritte had built for himself in Brussels; the butterfly represents myself. I love the idea of him rolling the carpet back after dinner, bringing out his easel and paints, and then rolling the carpet back when he had finished.

I have always admired the work of Joseph Cornell, although it has not been that great of an influence on me. We have both worked with the box format, and in this sense I owe a great deal to Cornell. I have done a self-portrait in which I am looking out of the window in my house in New Haven, across Long Island Sound, to Cornell's house in Queens.

The working process of making the objects has been, for me, extremely difficult, since I am not basically a carpenter or machinist. It is much easier for me to conceptualize and to lay the construction out than it is to put it together. For instance, it has taken me over a year to put up one shelf in my house. The difficult materials and tools such as epoxy, drills, saws, knives, and scissors present painful hazards. Certain constructions have taken a couple of weeks to put together because of the various stages, but it may have taken me years to find the material itself. Also, some objects may wait in my studio for twenty years before I find the right use for them in a construction. Sometimes a piece just will not resolve itself and will be put aside.

This morning in Lewisburg, Pennsylvania I began work on a new construction. I found four different objects while looking for antiques. When I excitedly brought them back to my room, I lined the children's blocks up on the desk, shuffled them around, and asked whether I had a major piece here or a minor piece.

I hope that the works will evoke in the audience the type of feeling that I get not only when I find the materials, but the excitement I feel putting them together and realizing that I have something that is quite satisfactory to the goals and standards which I have set for myself. It is my desire that the viewer will relate to certain things, possibly things played with as a child or things they now own.

3
RAMBO AND THE MYTH OF REDEMPTION

ROBERT JEWETT and JOHN SHELTON LAWRENCE

Introduction

The evolution of a culture is constituted in part by alterations in its story forms and significant texts. One of the oldest and most frequently transformed texts in world literature is the story of redemption from captivity. In America, tales of captivity have been our dominant national story form (Slotkin 1973). In contemporary popular entertainments from *Star Trek* to *Rambo*, we find a scheme featuring the rescue of innocent captives by superheroic means. Our news media are equally committed to stories of captivity. Consider the following symptomatic television vignette: At the end of the TWA Flight 847 captivity (July 1985, Lebanon), ABC television offered a live broadcast of a banquet featuring the TWA hostages and their Shiite guards—a meal crowned by a sponge cake dessert with large letters spelling "WISHING YOU ALL A HAPPY TRIP HOME." No event in the history of unconventional warfare has had a more made-for-media quality. News analysts who object to this preoccupation with hostage stories have invented sarcastic phrases such as "prime time terrorism," "grabbing the U.S. by the networks," and "hijacking the media."

When our film industry and news media are so dedicated to the captivity story, it should not be surprising that national leaders lose their balance in dealing with captivities. Jimmy Carter and Ronald Reagan both damaged their presidencies in attempting to deal with hostage situations. President Carter held one hundred crisis sessions of the National Security Council during the first one hundred and eighty days of the Iranian situation (Oberdorfer 1981, 38). By 1986, President Reagan, who rode the discontent with Carter's hostage policies into office, had allowed his own administration to stumble on the captivity issue.

Promising "swift and effective retribution" against terrorists during his campaign, he directed his state department to announce, "Terrorists can expect no concessions from us. We will not pay ransom or release prisoners. We will not bargain for the release of hostages" (Salinger 1981, 2). Soon after the discovery that these widely supported policies had been violated, a presidential aide revealed that "President Reagan was so anxious to free the American hostages in Lebanon that he spent 50 percent of his morning briefings discussing the hostages and was willing to secretly reverse American law and to supply Iran with American military equipment 'as a demonstration of good faith' if that would help free them" (Bernard Gwertzman 1986, 7). Oliver North also related that "With the president . . . it always came back to the hostages" and that "it was a terrible mistake to say that the president wanted a strategic relationship with Iran, because the president wanted the hostages" (Marz 1987, 25).

The question is why recent American presidents, goaded by public pressure, have allowed themselves to become so preoccupied with hostage crises. The puzzle is deepened by comparison with other countries like Italy, France, Great Britain, Germany, and Czechoslovakia, who have handled hostage situations with less fanfare and governmental paralysis.

We suggest that some answers lie in our tradition of the captivity story. We believe that American public consciousness has been shaped by a peculiar national legacy in which classical and biblical narratives of captivity were transformed into mass entertainments and public news rituals. These have had a significant effect on the perception of the world shared by presidents and public alike.

We begin our sketch of antecedents for "America Held Hostage in Iran/Lebanon" with classical stories of captivity, then turn to the biblical tradition and its influence upon the interpretation of conflicts between settlers and Indians.

Classical Stories of Captivity

Captivity and escape are among the oldest human concerns. From earliest civilizations, slavery threatened men, women, and children alike. Apart from such political dangers, bondage provided a recurrent theme for storytellers. The great epic poets of the ancient world, Homer and Virgil, gave captivity episodes a central place in the adventures of Odysseus and Aeneas. The political captivities of the Israelites in Egypt and in Babylon are key national episodes in the Old Testament. Captivities were recurrent themes among the folktales of the European tradition. In all these sources, captivities are much more than entertaining heroic narratives. They are laden with deeply felt moral and political attitudes.

As a framework for analysis, we suggest that classical materials conform to the model of the "monomyth" described by Joseph Campbell in his book *The Hero with a Thousand Faces*. He shows that the paradigm for thousands of primitive and classical folktales is based upon rites of initiation. The "classical monomyth" is a story of human maturation and integration in which the hero leaves home in search of adventure, slays a dragon, and then returns. His condensed statement of the paradigm runs as follows: "A hero ventures forth from the world of common day into a region of supernatural wonder: fabulous forces are there encountered and a decisive victory is won: the hero comes back from this mysterious initiation with the power to bestow boons on his fellow man" (Campbell 1956, 30). We schematically represent the classical story pattern with this diagram:

	Departure of the hero	
HOME: Permanent social and familial responsibilities	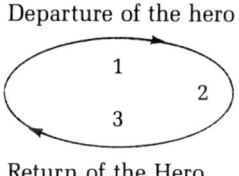	Encounter with fabulous dangers Victory
	Return of the Hero	

The point of departing from home in these classical tales is to grow up in the face of external threats. Once the trials have been mastered, the hero or heroine returns to normality. One marries, accepts communal leadership, raises a family, and thus assumes responsibility for the next generation.

Homer's Odyssey

Homer's great story of Odysseus's adventures conforms to the classical monomyth and makes liberal use of captivity themes as a means of exploring character. Odysseus makes war and wanders far from home for twenty years. Although he is a victim of the gods' quarrels about his fate, the prolonged dawdling corresponds to uncertainties about his life tasks. The captivities illustrate Odysseus's moral dilemmas, resources, and limitations. Each of his three captivities reveals him confronting a challenge thought to be typical for human development in the ancient world: the violent encounter with Cyclops and the prolonged erotic romances with Calypso and Circe.

Odysseus and his men naively wander onto the Cyclops's island after admiring the lushness of its vegetation and game. They begin to take what pleases them and are trapped in a cave with an ogre who rewards their greed by feasting upon them two at a time. By a combination of ruses, physical courage in plunging a smoldering log into Polyphemus's eye, and wiliness in sneaking out with the sheep, Odysseus and a few of his men survive. As Odysseus recounts it:

> I kept thinking how to win the game:
> death sat there huge; how could we slip away?
> I drew on all my wits, and ran through tactics,
> reasoning as a man will for dear life,
> until a trick came—and it pleased me well.
> (9. 420–24; Fitzgerald 1962, 157)

But in his escape, Odysseus cannot resist a foolish taunting of the Cyclops—against the advice of his men—in the moment of their escape. He later confesses the hubris expressed in this taunt:

> I would not heed them in my glorying spirit,
> but let my anger flare and yelled . . .
> Odysseus, raider of cities, took your eye.
> (9.500–5; Fitzgerald 1962, 160)

Odysseus's ship is almost destroyed when half a mountain is hurled in the direction of this proud voice.

The adventures in the warm, comfortable dwellings of Calypso and Circe show us a man captivated, not by terror, but by sensual temptation. Calypso is a mistress of enchantment, and Odysseus is profoundly tempted by her promise. In his words,

> The enchantress in her beauty
> fed and caressed me, promised me I should be
> immortal, youthful, all the days to come;
> but in my heart I never gave consent
> though seven years detained.
> (7.250–55; Fitzgerald 1962, 118)

Homer's voice suggests the critical attitude of the classical world concerning the dangers of sexual attraction and of a passive life:

> The sweet days of his life time
> were running out in anguish over his exile,
> for long ago the nymph had ceased to please.
> Though he fought shy of her and her desire,
> he lay with her each night, for she compelled him.
> (5.150–53; Fitzgerald 1962, 85)

The lovely companion had "ceased to please"—meaning, of course, that Odysseus had once seriously considered immortal sexual bliss with her. Yet he finds the pleasures increasingly empty and inconsistent with his need to return to his own family and community. He frees himself ultimately, not by violence or divine invocation, but through his repeated affirmation to Calypso that he cannot find his fulfillment there with her. Having demonstrated this point through speech and weeping, sullen behavior, he finally gains divine permission to depart. Further into the Homeric narrative, Odysseus encounters another divine and magical lady, Circe, who detains him as her consort in her "flawless bed of love" (10.347; Fitzgerald 1962, 176). Once again, Odysseus must struggle against sexual temptation to regain control of his life's journey. Homer ends the episode with one more resonant parallel on the temptation theme: Odysseus and his men cannot compel themselves to follow Circe's instructions on avoiding the dangers of the Sirens. They nearly perish.

Virgil and Aeneas

Virgil's great epic, The Aeneid, contains a comparable test for Aeneas in the court of Queen Dido of Carthage. She rescues Aeneas and his men by allowing them to land on her shores and to enjoy friendly hospitality in her court. She and Aeneas are mutually attracted by one another's physical beauty and personal warmth. They experience a kind of natural marriage in a cave and become devoted lovers. Immersed in sexual pleasure, Aeneas forgets his mission to found a great city until the alarmed Jove sends Mercury with an urgent message: "Are you now laying the foundations of lofty Carthage and a slave to your wife, building a beautiful city, forgetful, alas, of your kingdom and your own affairs?" (Guinagh 1953, 91). With mixed feelings about his task and a great feeling of compassion for Dido, he resolves to leave and asks that his men be allowed to repair the ships so that they can sail toward Latium. Dido wants to forbid or subvert their departure, but Aeneas's firmness carries them away.

In these classical stories, as in tales such as "Little Red Riding Hood" and "Hansel and Gretel," there is a structure of temptation, danger, escape, and return to traditional responsibilities. Redemption from captivity depends upon insight into self, an increased understanding of danger, and the exercise of courage. While the gods intervene frequently, human strength, wit, and moral resolution are essential to escaping bondage. The tension between immediate sensual pleasures and long-term communal responsibilities is played out in manifold ways. In Campbell's sense, these are monomythic tales in which individuals achieve the seasoned strength and wisdom required by the communities to which they return.

Captivity in the Old Testament

A more theocentric narrative of redemption emerges from the biblical accounts of captivity in Egypt and Babylon. The initiative and the act of redemption in both instances feature Yahweh as the primary actor rather than Moses or the Israelites themselves. The biblical stories thus glorify God as the "Divine Warrior" (Anderson 1975, 48).

The sojourn of the Israelite people in Egypt was the consequence of Joseph's invitation to his brothers to come for aid during a famine. Their status was that of laborers, not slaves. The rise of oppressive conditions is explained in Exodus 1:8–14 as a combination of governmental change and the fear of Israel's reproduction rate. Repressive working conditions and population control are depicted as the expression of imperial power. Yet the only resistance to the state depicted early in the Exodus story is from the midwives who refuse to kill the male children (Exodus 1:15–22) and the women of Moses' family who hide the infant in the bulrushes where he was discovered and raised by Pharaoh's daughter. Moses grows up as an Israelite bearing an Egyptian name, an outsider figure who identifies strongly with his oppressed kinfolk. After murdering an Egyptian taskmaster who is beating a Hebrew worker, Moses becomes a refugee in Midian.

In response to Israelites groaning under bondage, Yahweh appears to Moses in the burning bush and announces his purpose to deliver them. The element of divine initiative indicates that Yahweh is the real hero of the Exodus story:

> Then the Lord said, "I have seen the affliction of my people who are in Egypt, and have heard their cry because of their taskmasters; I know their sufferings, and I have come down to deliver them out of the hand of the Egyptians, and to bring them up out of that land to a good and broad land, a land flowing with milk and honey. . . . Come, I will send you to Pharaoh that you may bring forth my people, the sons of Israel, out of Egypt." (Exodus 3:7–10)

With great reluctance Moses becomes the agent of the divine compassion to set free the oppressed. In a series of ten dramatic struggles with Pharaoh, culminating in the Passover, Moses and his brother Aaron seek to compel Pharaoh to fear Yahweh sufficiently to grant freedom to the Israelites. Each time the promise of freedom is repudiated, while the oppressive conditions worsen. The repetitive hardening of Pharaoh's heart conveys the sense of bondage to arbitrary imperial power, while the ultimate triumph of Yahweh shows the limits of such power.

The escape from Egypt occurs on the night when the angel of Yahweh killed the first born of all houses not marked with the blood of the passover lamb. Pharaoh relents and allows the unprepared Israelites to flee into the wilderness. The element of divine intervention downplays any human participation: "And on that very day Yahweh brought the people of Israel out of the land of Egypt" (Exodus 12:51). This sense of the miraculous rescue of passive victims is heightened by the dramatic confrontation with Pharaoh's chariots, sent out to recapture the fugitives after the king changes his mind a final time. Moses reassures them:

> "Fear not, stand firm, and see the salvation of the Lord, which he will work for you today.... Yahweh will fight for you, and you have only to be still." Yahweh said to Moses ... "Tell the people of Israel to go forward. Lift up your rod, and stretch out your hand over the sea and divide it, that the people of Israel may go on dry ground through the sea. And I will harden the hearts of the Egyptians, so that they shall go in after them and I will get glory over Pharaoh and all his host, his chariots, and his horsemen." (Exodus 14:13–17)

The terrified Israelites do as they are told, striding between the walls of water and then watching as the pursuing Egyptians are drowned. The celebration initiated by Moses' sister, Miriam, articulates the essence of this miraculous rescue effected by a divine hero: "Sing to Yahweh, for he has triumphed gloriously; the horse and his rider he has thrown into the sea!" (Exodus 15:21).

In place of an escape of highly motivated and transformed individuals, as in the classical Greek and Roman narratives, here we encounter the miraculous rescue of powerless victims and, simultaneously, the formation of a new nation out of a formless mass of refugees. Imperial power rather than personal temptation, as with Odysseus and Aeneas, creates the focus for action. Michael Walzer conveys a clear grasp of this aspect of the exodus story, which has had such wide-ranging impact on American culture:

> We can think of the Exodus as an example of what is today called "national liberation." The people as a whole are enslaved, and then the people as a whole are delivered. At the same time, however, the

uses of the story . . . suggest that the Egyptian model reaches to every sort of oppression and to every sort of liberation. Perhaps the crucial point is the linking of oppression and state power. . . . Hence the escape from bondage is also the defeat of a tyrant—and the escape is only possible because of the defeat. (Walzer 1985, 32)

While this deliverance from tyrannical oppression required limited human participation, subsequent events in the Exodus story demand discipline and the character to form a new nation. The trials and temptations of classical captivity tales are transposed, so to speak, to the period after deliverance.

The forty-year test in the desert involved a number of components crucial for later Israelite consciousness. Living on the manna of the desert, which had to be gathered daily and could not be preserved, involved faith in Yahweh's provision and avoidance of the accumulation of possessions that might destroy an egalitarian people. Resisting the yearning for the "fleshpots" and secure gods of Egypt involved overcoming ideological and material temptations from an imperial civilization. In Michael Walzer's words, "the great paradox of the Exodus, and all of subsequent liberation struggles, is the people's simultaneous willingness and unwillingness to put Egypt behind them" (73). The severe conditions in the desert revealed the shortcomings of all human leaders, including Moses and his family, contrasted with the faithfulness of Yahweh. Ultimately the entire Exodus generation of former slaves would have to perish before the Promised Land could be won. A newly disciplined and obedient generation for whom Egypt no longer comprised a nostalgic memory was required to effect the final transition from liberation to nationhood.

The central event in the desert period was the covenant at Mount Sinai, in which Yahweh revealed the commandments and Israel committed itself to obedience: "All that Yahweh has spoken we will do" (Exodus 19:8). Here the moral laws are conceived as derived not from an earthly leader or tradition but directly from God who has redeemed his people. All become responsible for keeping this covenant (Kaufmann 1960, 233). Women and children, leaders and followers, are included within a radically inclusive social ideal. The centrality of this covenant in the Exodus narrative and in later Israelite—and American—

consciousness is conveyed by the fact that the remaining portion of the book of Exodus, the entirety of Leviticus, and the first ten chapters of Numbers deal with the legal details and later events associated with Sinai. The consequence is that obedience to covenant obligations is construed as the form of maturity required for successful nationhood, while moral and ideological faults come to be understood as betrayal of the covenant. Disloyalty to the national values is thus interpreted as worshipping the false gods and values of foreign cultures; ideological and moral adherence to the covenant becomes the crucial corollary of redemption from Egyptian bondage.

In the drama of subsequent Israelite history this scheme of covenantal loyalty assumes the central role. Disobedience is interpreted as resulting in foreign triumphs over Israel, while repentance and renewal of covenantal commitment brings Yahweh's renewed intervention on behalf of Israel. This paradigm manifests itself in the understanding of the Babylonian captivity that commenced in the sixth century B.C.E. It was seen as a punishment for the lack of ideological purity and fidelity to the moral legacy of Israel's faith (See 2 Kings 24:9–10). Elements of imprudent zeal are visible in the account of Israel's fateful rebellion against Babylon, but the punishments scheme remained dominant. The deportation to Babylon resulted in a renewed period of ideological temptation and humiliation. Israel once again found itself in captivity, this time because of its own sins.

The rescue from Babylonian captivity was interpreted as a kind of second exodus in which Yahweh symbolically repeated his exploit of drying up the sea so that "the redeemed" could pass over (Isaiah 51:10). In this instance the release of the captives occurred politically through King Cyrus, who came to power in Babylon. His ascendancy and the promulgation of his policy of returning captives to their homeland were viewed as a miraculous intervention of Yahweh who had made Cyrus his unknowing "shepherd" (Isaiah 44:28) and "messiah" (Isaiah 45:1). We encounter here a paradigm different from the classical monomyth: superhuman redemption of faithful or unfaithful victims, whose maturity is required not before but after their rescue from bondage. Here maturity is interpreted primarily in ideological and moral categories: maintaining internal justice and refusing obeisance to foreign gods. The following summarizes these relationships with a second paradigm statement and schematic representation:

> The Exodus Paradigm: "A community with a prior experience of freedom falls under foreign oppression: it is rescued by a deity whom it then covenants to obey: forged by testing and obedience to the wilderness, the nation gains a promised land where its future depends on continued loyalty."

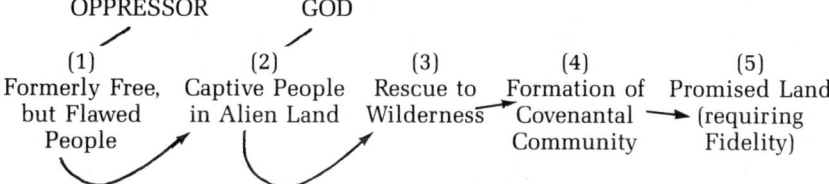

It is this celebration of captivity and rescue, rather than the classical model of captivity and escape, that seems to predominate in American culture (Reinhold 1984, 236–41, 307–9) leading from the earliest Indian captivity narratives down to *Rambo*. The Bible provides the primary matrix of redemption in American culture, into which elements of the classical monomyth are occasionally incorporated.

Captivity in the American National Experience

The American national experience provided many occasions to reflect on the stories of the captive Israelites. From the earliest settlement of the New World by Europeans, the Indians took captives. Thousands were taken, whether from motives of revenge, ransom, leverage for treaty negotiation, or to replace tribal members lost to disease or warfare. The first of the accounts written by an American was Mary Rowlandson's *The Sovereignty and Goodness of God . . . A Narrative of . . . Captivity and Restoration . . .* , which appeared in 1682. The description of her capture, suffering, and eventual escape marked the beginning of an almost inexhaustible genre in American letters. Her book had appeared in thirty editions by 1900 and was followed by other personal memoirs describing similar experiences, such as John Williams's *The Redeemed Captive Returning to Zion* (1706).

American captivity narratives expressed the Puritan adaptation of the biblical captivity narrative for the American scene. Roy Harvey Pearce suggested that the captivity story is a "popular form which shapes and reshapes itself according to varying immediate cultural 'needs.'" (Pearce 1949, 1). The Puritan accounts of captivity reflect the preoccupation with purity of conscience and often emphasize elements of "spiritual autobiography" (Levernier and Cohen 1977, 32). Captives like Mary Rowlandson saw the providential though chastening hand of God at work in their experiences. Although the Indians were, in Mary Rowlandson's graphic words, "a company of hell-hounds, roaring, singing, ranting and insulting" (Lincoln 1913, 120–21), they were instrumental to an ordeal set in motion by Providence; in reconstructing each stage of her experience, she could find a scriptural parallel to her circumstance that informed her of God's punishing but benevolently instructive will. Like other introspective Puritans seized by Indians, she saw her captivity experience as the divine judgment upon herself and her society for its spiritual sloth. "And I hope I can say in some measure, as David did, It is good for me that I have been afflicted. The Lord hath shewed me the vanity of these outward things. That they are the Vanity of vanities, and vexation of the spirit" (Lincoln 1913, 167). The individual or the community that had fallen into "vanities" deserved terror in the wilderness. Her husband's accompanying sermon—"The Possibility of God's Forsaking a People that have been near and dear to Him"—embodies this theme as did John Williams's *Redeemed Captive* (1706). The latter wrote, "our perverse and evil carriages in the sight of the Lord have so offended him, that instead of turning his hand against them [the Indians], the Lord nourishes them up to be a scourge to the whole land." And like an Old Testament prophet, he lamented the sinfulness of mere ritual in religion, complaining that "Days of Fasting and Prayer, without REFORMATION, will not avail to turn away the Anger of God from a Professing People" (Vaughn and Clark 1981, 9).

Cotton Mather, the foremost creator of captivity jeremiads, stated that making public "the terrible and barbarous Things undergone by some of our English Captives in the Hands of the Eastern Indians" would "promote the general Repentance" and "give Testimony to the Justice and Goodness of our Lord Jesus Christ" (Levernier and Cohen 1977, 31). One of the clearest examples of this ritual moralizing is the sermon on Hannah Swarton's captivity contained in Mather's volume *Humiliations Followed by Deliverances* (1697). She had lost her husband and three of her children through the encounter with the Indians and concluded, with Mather's emphatic insistence, that her experience had resulted from moving too far from the ethos of Puritan social control.

> My sins had been a burden to me: I desired to see all of my Sins, and to repent of them all with my Heart, and of that Sin which had been especially a Burden to me: namely, That I Left the Publick Worship and Ordinances of God, to go to live in a remote Place, without the Publick Ministry; depriving our selves and our Children of so great a benefit for our souls; and all this for worldly advantages." (Levernier and Cohen 1977, 38)

These words, which were delivered by Mather in the presence of Mrs. Swarton, clearly illustrate the social purpose to which an alert, ecclesiastical mind could turn the unfortunate experiences of the captives. The norm of convenantal fidelity is very explicit here.

But after a century of captivity tales, the conscience-stricken, biblically referenced view had weakened. The "land imperative" (Levernier and Cohen, 1977) had become a more dominant theme in the narratives by the late eighteenth century. In addition to continuing the excoriation of the Indian, accounts of captivity now also served the purpose of arousing sentiment against French competitors for the American territory. Details were often included indicating the fertility and promise of the land yet to be taken. In this more secular, propagandistic vein, the title of Peter Williamson's *French and Indian cruelty; exemplified in the life and various vicissitudes of fortune, of Peter Williamson* (1757) makes clear the political (as opposed to spiritual) concern, and also betrays a new interest in the sensational, heroic experience of an individual person. Whereas the Puritan narratives had generally contained titles glorifying God's power and mercy to deliver the chastened captive—as with Elizabeth Hanson's *God's Mercy Surmounting Man's Cruelty* (1728) or Jonathan Dickenson's *God's Protecting Providence Man's Surest Help and Defence* (1699), the diminishing power of Puritan theology was accompanied by the search for remarkable heroes with sensational, this-worldly experiences. The notion that God will redeem repentant captives by mysterious agencies gave way to a hope for heroic human redeemers who could outthink and outfight the wicked foe.

The deletion of the spiritual or cultural self-criticism was consistent with the accelerating expansionist social agenda of American society in the late eighteenth and nineteenth centuries. Of course, even when the spiritual framework remained, cultural extermination of the Indian was a prominent leitmotif. To Cotton Mather, almost every fragment of information about white experiences of captivity proved the Indians' intransigent evil and established a divine mandate (while provoking a helping hand) for their extermination. In his *Decennium Luctuosum* (1699), he stated, "The evident hand of Heaven appearing on the Side of a people whose Hope and Help was alone in the Almighty Lord of Hosts, Extinguished whole Nations of the Salvages at such a rate, that there can hardly any of them now be found under any Distinction upon the face of the Earth" (Lincoln 1913, 184). This cultural mandate survived the secularization of Puritan society. By the nineteenth century, the destroying Providence of the Puritans had been replaced by "laws of progress." In 1877 Richard Irving Dodge wrote that "the Indians will as surely disappear before the progress of the more energetic and aggressive Anglo-Saxon, as the snows of winter melt away before the summer sun." Dodge was consoled by the knowledge that "the savage is giving way to a higher and more civilized race" (Dodge 1877, liv). For a culture largely bent upon destroying the Indians, this theme of inevitable, providential progress eroded attention to the historical complexity of the tragic interaction between whites and Indians. It also prevented acknowledgment of the ethical power in the Indians' way of life.

The extermination of the Indian was celebrated even more often in the mass pulp literature that developed in the nineteenth century. In inexpensive "dime novels," the first mass-produced and nationally distributed literature in the United States, Indian captivity established itself as a favored theme. Edward Ellis's *Seth Jones, or The Captives of the Frontier* (1861) was issued in nine separate editions and eventually had a circulation of four hundred thousand. Ellis followed with many other novels embodying themes of captivity, rescue, and revenge: *Nathan Todd, or The Fate of the Sioux Captive* (1861); *White Slayer, the Avenger, or The Doomed Redskins*. Percy St. John wrote *The Queen of the Woods, or The Shawnee Captive* (1868), and Joseph Badger wrote *The Forest Princess, or The Kickapoo Captive* (1871). These popular novels developed the idea of heroic rescue by frontiersmen and cowboys.

In choosing a representative example from the nineteenth-century captivity materials, we are guided by our interest in a story type that evolves toward our present national preoccupation with hostages. A significant example is a well-known sculpture of Horatio Greenough, *The Rescue* (1837), which was placed at the Capitol building in Washington, D.C. Greenough remarked, "I have endeavoured to convey the idea of the triumph of the whites over the savage tribes, at the same time that it illustrates the danger of peopling the country" (Wright 1972, 221). His sentiments were like those of most writers or artists who sought to recreate for fellow citizens the experience of captivity, of Indian savagery, and the resulting need for whites to triumph over them. With few exceptions, the outpouring of books, pulp novels, and later films and television dramas conveyed the same message.

What we inherited from the Indian captivity tradition was a cluster of perceptions consisting of: (1) a simplistic moral polarization into a world with innocent victims representing civilization and villains who stand for aggressive barbarism; (2) a resulting formula for the conflict between aggressor and victim that suppresses relevant facts; (3) an emotional imperative for rescue or retribution, at whatever cost in life, legality, or national interest; and (4) an expectation of miraculous circumstances or powers that can achieve redemption of captives despite all odds.

The captivity story also laid the foundation for a new kind of hero, which can best be described as a superheroic variant of the classical monomyth. The following is a paradigm statement and its schematic correlate:

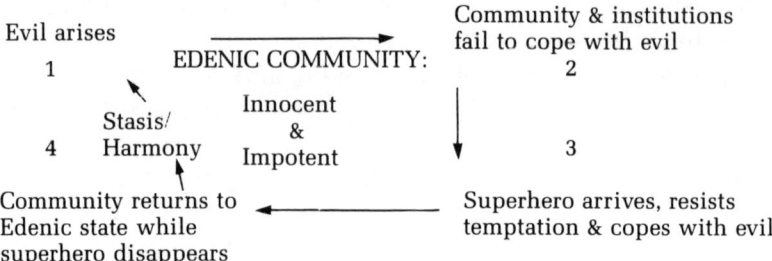

The American Monomyth Paradigm: "A community in a harmonious paradise is threatened by evil: normal institutions fail to deal with this threat: a selfless superhero emerges to renounce temptations and carry out the redemptive task: aided by fate, his decisive victory restores the community to its paradisal condition: the superhero then recedes into obscurity." (Jewett and Lawrence 1977, xx)

Rambo and the Contemporary Captivity Narrative

Some of the most powerful embodiments of the American monomyth in contemporary mass culture have been created by Sylvester Stallone. He has sought to make himself a symbol of American power and patriotism, succeeding in a way that seems to confirm the legend of Rocky—the hopeless underdog who becomes a world champ. Recognizing his status as an American icon, *Newsweek* featured him, draped in the national flag, on its cover. Almost all of Stallone's films express his personal philosophy that violence must always be answered by greater violence. He has been welcomed at the White House, where the implicit message of his film *Rambo* was publicly praised by President Reagan. It is also clear that Stallone's films fit into a broader pattern that includes films like *Invasion USA*, *Red Dawn*, *Missing in Action*, *Commando*, and *Delta Force* and *Hanoi Hilton*. Since *Rambo* is one of the most successful films in history, revealing widespread cultural resonance, it expresses a cluster of values that are characteristic of America in the 1980s.

Rambo: First Blood, Part II is unusually clear in condensing and rehearsing the conventions of the American mythic tradition. John Rambo is an outsider figure with superhuman skills for killing and for rescuing the captives who have been abandoned by a corrupt democratic system. Only when he defies democratic authority can he save the POWs in Vietnam, and at long last symbolically win the war that was betrayed by political compromise. The film is filled with images of suffering—his and that of the innocent, helpless men he will rescue.

In the film's plot, Rambo is released from prison (after a prolonged episode of destroying an Oregon logging town in *First Blood*) on condition that he secretly photograph American captives at a hidden camp in Vietnam. He plaintively asks Colonel Trautman, "Sir, do we get to win the war this time?" and is satisfied with the answer that "It's up to you." He is dropped into the jungle where the POWs are being held. He discovers the camp, and, having lost his camera because of his superior's bureaucratic bungling, immediately rescues an American being tortured on a cross. When Rambo defies his orders by deciding to bring back the prisoners, the CIA officer aborts the mission and abandons them.

Rambo is thereupon captured by the Vietnamese and tortured on various cruciform devices, obviously suggesting the principal redemptive figure of Christian culture. These agonies are supervised by Soviet advisers, but through superhuman strength and the help of a Vietnamese girl he has befriended, he escapes. He becomes a one-man army, destroying the entire garrison of the torture camp and its Soviet reinforcements. He uses both bullet and arrow, true to the tradition of the frontiersman in the Indian captivity narrative and the *Leatherstocking Tales*. After the death of the beautiful, helpful Ca Ba, who makes the fateful mythic mistake of telling Rambo that she wants to go with him, Rambo commandeers an aged American helicopter and rescues the bedraggled and forgotten POWs. He must first gun down a sleek, advanced Soviet gunship that pursues him. When he returns to Thailand with the rescued men, he turns the M-60 machine gun from the aged chopper onto the computers and communications equipment that symbolize the corrupt command structure of a democratic army. He almost kills the cowardly officer who aborted his mission, but stops short after showing him menacing contempt. As in so many other adventure-fantasy films that fight the Vietnam War again, a single man symbolically accomplishes what years of massive governmental effort failed to do.

The mixed legacy of several captivity traditions is evident in this especially potent American mythic brew—but with radical foreshortenings of the apparent elements of wisdom in those traditions. From the classical tradition one finds the rejection of sexual temptation, even sexuality itself, but without its symbolic demands for maturation or acceptance of traditional communal and familial responsibility. From the Old Testament and Puritan stories of redemption survives the notion of an unworthy community that must repent after its rescue, but now absent is the imperative for fidelity to a disciplining covenant that demands democratic allegiance and conduct. What remains most evidently is the zealous, explosive belligerence from the Indian captivity story in its final expansionist phase. The new covenant, so to speak, is a narcissistic commitment to preserving a sense of righteous innocence and dominance in a world that persists in making its own demands for equity and justice. In its most outrageous fantasies, the myth betrays a yearning for superheroes to provide miraculous victories despite all the limiting circumstances or countervailing forces. A final paradigm statement and diagram summarizes the distinctive features of this story form.

> The *Rambo* Paradigm: "A world-dominant, democratic nation is defeated through its cowardly acceptance of limited, compromising goals—rather than persisting in zealous ideals: innocent victims remain in bondage to evil victors: since rescue by normal agencies is not feasible, a superwarrior emerges and is sent: despite an unscrupulous foe, incredible odds, and the betrayal by a corrupt leadership, the warrior rescues the captives: his triumph repudiates democratic weakness and erases the stigma of prior defeat: the indifferent community regains its former status while the superwarrior disappears."

Recognizing this peculiar constellation of mythic values in *Rambo* can help us interpret the behavior of the news media and of our recent American presidents. The prolonged fixation on the hostages and their suffering reaffirms the innocence of the

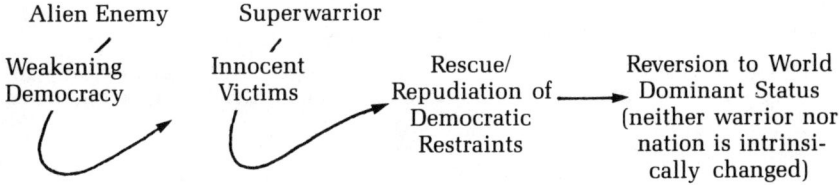

American people and the impotence of law and diplomacy. The coverage of hostage episodes from Iran (1979–81) provided emotional focus on American innocence and unjustified suffering.

The prevailing myth system makes it compelling for leaders fixated upon these images of innocent suffering to act outside the law, secretively, to create the mysterious conditions required for redemption. President Ford's impulsive behavior in the Mayaguez Incident (1975), President Carter's disastrous "Operation Blue Light" in the Iranian Desert (1980), and finally, President Reagan's alarming duplicities and oversights in Iran (1986) suggest a pattern of leadership far more deeply committed to the mythic imperatives of a story tradition than to the Constitution. Chafing discomforts with the rule of law are evident in the fact that when caught in the inconsistency between democratic ideals and zealous behavior, our national leaders dismiss such conduct as an unfortunate mistake, a risk worth taking again to save precious American lives.

Understanding the processes through which captivity texts are culturally transformed could contribute to moving beyond some of the current crises for democratic values. An important task of higher education is to offer students the resources to understand and to evaluate this process for themselves. In this sense, humanistic studies may offer the most promising resource for grasping and clarifying the values required for a democratic society.

Annotated Bibliography

[Items with an asterisk (*) have been cited in the text of the presentation.]

Classical Period

PRIMARY SOURCES

*Homer. *The Odyssey.* Translated by Robert Fitzgerald. Garden City, N.Y.: Anchor Books, Doubleday, 1963. Book IX relates the episode among the Cyclops; Books V and VII deal with Calypso; Book X with Circe.

*Virgil. *The Aeneid.* Translated by Kevin Guinagh. New York: Holt, Rinehart, 1953. Book IV relates Aeneas' romantic captivity with Dido.

*Hebrew Scripture/*Old Testament.* Exodus 1–15 deals with the Egyptian captivity, while Isaiah 40–55 and 2 Chronicles 36 deal with the Babylonian.

COMMENTARY SOURCES

*Anderson, Bernhard W. *Understanding the Old Testament.* 3d ed. Englewood Cliffs, N.J.: Prentice Hall, 1975.

Bettelheim, Bruno. *The Uses of Enchantment: The Meaning and Importance of Fairy Tales.* New York: Knopf, 1977. Discusses stories that invite reflection on anxieties and the symbolic means of moving beyond them.

*Campbell, Joseph. *The Hero with a Thousand Faces.* New York: Meridian, 1956.

Greenberg, Moshe. *Understanding Exodus.* New York: Behrman, 1969.

Humphreys, W. Lee. *Crisis and Story: Introduction to the Old Testament.* Palo Alto, Calif.: Mayfield, 1979.

*Jewett, Robert, and John S. Lawrence. *The American Monomyth.* Garden City, N.Y.: Anchor Books, Doubleday, 1977. Develops a distinction between classical myths of discovery and maturation and the later American myths of redemption.

*Kaufmann, Yehezkel. *The Religion of Israel: From Its Beginnings to the Babylonian Exile.* Translated by M. Greenberg. Chicago: University of Chicago Press, 1960.

Neumann, Erich. *The Origins and History of Consciousness.* Princeton, N.J.: Princeton University Press, 1954. The chapter "The Captive and the Treasure" deals with the theme of maturation from a Jungian point of view.

Reinhold, Meyer. *Classica Americana: The Greek and Roman Heritage in the United States.* Detroit, Mich.: Wayne State University Press, 1984. A definitive study of the use of classical materials in American literature.

*Walzer, Michael. *Exodus and Revolution.* New York: Basic Books, 1985.

American Indian Captivities

Berkhofer, Robert. *The White Man's Indian: Images of the American Indian from Columbus to Present.* New York: Knopf, 1978.

*Dodge, Richard Irving. *The Plains of the Great West and their Inhabitants, Being a Description of Plains, Game, Indians & of the Great North American Desert.* New York: Putnam, 1877.

*Levernier, James, and Hennig Cohen. *The Indians and Their Captives.* Westport, Conn.: Greenwood Press, 1977. A collection of captivities from different periods in American history.

*Lincoln, Charles H., ed. *Narratives of the Indian Wars: 1675–1679.* New York: Scribner's, 1913.

*Pearce, Roy Harvey. "The Significances of the Captivity Narrative." *American Literature* 19 (1947): 1–20. One of the first interpreters to recognize the culturally plastic quality of the narratives.

Slotkin, Richard. *Regeneration Through Violence: The Mythology of the American Frontier, 1600–1860. Middletown, Conn.: Wesleyan University Press, 1973. A book with chapters on the scriptural analogies through which Puritans interpreted their experience in "the howling wilderness" and their captivities among Indians.

Strong, Pauline Turner. "Captive Images." Natural History, 12 (1985): 52–57. Includes a careful analysis of the ideological function of captivity during the Indian wars of the late 18th century.

*Vail, R.W.G. The Voice of the Old Frontier. Philadelphia: University of Pennsylvania Press, 1949. A bibliography of publications in the United States prior to 1800; it contains significant annotations on early captivity narratives.

Van der Beets, Richard. Held Captive by Indians. Knoxville: University of Tennessee Press, 1973. An historically balanced collection of narratives.

*Vaughan, Alden T., and Edward Clark, eds. Puritans among the Indians: Accounts of Captivity and Redemption, 1676–1724. Cambridge, Mass.: Harvard University Press, 1981. An excellent collection of Puritan captivities with fine commentaries.

Washburn, Wilcomb, ed. Narratives of North American Indian Captivities. New York: Garland Reprint Series, 1978. A collection of 311 captivities in 111 volumes. The series drew upon the collection of more than one thousand captivity narratives in the Newberry Library of Chicago.

*Wright, Nathalia. Letters of Horatio Greenough American Sculptor. Madison: University of Wisconsin Press, 1972.

Contemporary Period

Ascenio, Diego, and Nancy Ascenio. Our Man Is Inside. Boston, Mass.: Little & Brown, 1983. An account of an American diplomat's captivity among members of Columbia's M–19 revolutionary group. This case was handled with little ideological fanfare.

Bucher, Lloyd. My Story. Garden City, N.Y.: Doubleday, 1970. A personal account of the Pueblo Incident that occurred in 1968 off the shore of North Korea. Bucher was court-martialed upon returning. The military men, who had surrendered, were not lionized as heroes.

Ford, Gerald R. A Time to Heal. New York: Harper & Row, 1979. The former president's account of his excitement about the morale-building aspects of the Mayaguez episode.

*Gwertzman, Bernard. "Why President Ended Silence on Iran Policy." New York Times, 14 November 1986, p. 7.

*Marz, Larry, et al. "Going Nowhere Fast." Newsweek, 9 February 1987, p. 25.

*Oberdorfer, Don. "Now That It's Over . . . The Press Needs to Reflect on Its Role." Washington Journalism Review, May 1981, pp. 37–38.

Rowan, Roy. The Four Days of Mayaguez. New York: Norton, 1975. An enthusiastic journalistic account of the Mayaguez episode.

*Salinger, Pierre. America Held Hostage: The Secret Negotiations. Garden City, N.Y.: Doubleday, 1981. An extensive journalistic account with surprising revelations about secrecy within the Carter administration.

4
"IT WAS ULYSSES AND IT WAS NOT": TRADITIONAL REFRACTIONS

JOHN WHEATCROFT

I

We are creatures of predicament. Our partaking of predicament is not only constant but varied. No need to catalog the seemingly endless number and kinds of predicaments in which we find ourselves and by which we define our existence. These range from the most sweeping geopolitical and public to the most intensely psychological and private, from the largest conceptions we can form of nebulae, quasars, black holes, and antimatter to our intimations of the most minute particles—which also seem to lead us to a Balboa-like perspective on antiuniverse or antibeing. Such predications are a bit scary, at least for those of us who profess the human arts.

The particular human predicament I want to consider in this essay may be viewed as more obvious, evident, and immediate, yet just as inscrutable, perplexing, and elusive as black holes and antimatter. I am concerned with time. My inclinations are not metaphysical. On that side of the concept St. Augustine stated that if you don't ask me what time is, I know perfectly well. However if you ask me, I really can't tell you.

To be sure, there is a difference between time, whatever it is, and the conception, ways of measuring, ways of valuing time different peoples and cultures have. The second are relative. Perhaps because in our latitudes sunlight, warmth, and the growing season are limited and short, we see time as a scarce commodity and hence come to say time is money and we behave as if it were. Such a notion may well be the source of and the nourishment for our competitiveness and for our making work a moral imperative. Perhaps, too, our sense of scarcity creates anxiety in us that causes us to mourn the past and to be apprehensive about the possibilities of time to come. The concept of time we have formed and by which we live is exhaustible and linear. Under the influence of Christian eschatology as it combined with Enlightenment rationalism and science, within time we have traditionally held to a causational view of human experience, and we have thought in terms of beginnings, middles, and ends. Ours has been a most time-anxious and teleological ethos.

Granted, all peoples are not so deeply obsessed by or neurotic about temporality as we are. There is an aspect of time, however, that, apart from relative senses of it, seems to be a common denominator: the human awareness of mortality. I would guess that even those languages without tense have formed some symbolic means for signifying "before I was" and "after I am not." All creatures conscious of their predicament, it would seem, because of their recognition of the limitation on their living, define themselves by marking off or drawing the lines of their being in temporal terms.

Most peoples have dealt with this awareness of limitation in two ways. First, they have expanded themselves to take in units larger than the separate consciousness—family, clan, tribe, nation, civilization, culture. Perhaps it is fear of difficulty in accepting the idea of extinction as individual that compels us to consider and partake of the larger, more durable group. Hence we celebrate our forebears and hope for offspring. It seems that the more we are able to incorporate the larger and longer into our preciously limited selves, the less our vulnerability to limitation possesses and spoils our presentness.

The recognition we call memory, in the form of genealogical catalogs, annals, chronicles, history, sacred writings, literature, and music, as well as such iconography as barrows, tombs, stelae, reliquaries, sculpture, architecture, painting, photography, allows us to inform our always-dying present with some of the significant past. On the other side, our ability to project hope and fear in the form of our imaginings, envisionings, and shrinkings, our construction of utopias, heavens, and hells, these permit us to inform our always-being-born present with some of the significant future. In respect to this expansion of our awareness of before and after into a larger dimension, our predicament is that our present is invaded from two directions, there are conflicting claims on our now. We feel impelled to escape from the catch of limited, encroaching time by entering some moment of cultural wholeness.

The second way in which we deal with this elemental awareness of the limitation of our beingness is to contract it into an endurable tension within our individual consciousness in the now. To write and to read, to speak and to listen, is to move through time in words. To use language is to employ symbolic means of infusing the present with the past and the future. Our individual predicament also is that we feel the tug of both by the then and the to-come, of the old and the new, of the conservative and the progressive (in the literal, nonpolitical sense of these words), on our conscious present.

As with family and culture, it would seem that the more of "was" and "will be" we are able to incorporate into our present instant of individual being, without overwhelming it, the more we enrich our beingness. I suspect, too, that our equilibrium is determined by our ability to adjudicate and balance between the conflicting claims. Again, a great deal of relativism, cultural and genetic, exists, making absolute notions of proportion an undesirability as well as an impossibility. Yet, whatever the amount and balance, our awareness of our temporal limitation, of our finiteness, draws us toward the infinite both as members of a society and as individuals. "In ultimate truth," writes George Steiner in "The Retreat from the Word," "past, present, and future are simultaneously comprised."

To be sure, the present instant, which is gone even before we can name or refer to it, always eludes us. The Swiss artist Paul Klee writes in his diary: "Time ticks and ticks, and the pen has already been dipped." Yet after any given moment has gone and before it arrives, we can predicate it. The past, irretrievable as it is, and the future, which cannot be entered until it is no longer future, also can be signified. It is not by naming them we possess or control them. Rather, it is by naming them that we conceive of or define our momentary beingness, we construct ourselves. Not to do so would seem to threaten our sense of our existence. In *The Sense of an Ending*, historian Frank Kermode informs us that "the physician Alkmeon observed, with Aristotle's approval, that men die because they cannot join the beginning and the end." The Israeli theologian and philosopher Martin Buber puts it this way in *I and Thou*: "One cannot live in the pure present; it would consume us if care were not taken that it is overcome quickly and thoroughly." To repeat my initial proposition, we are creatures of predicament both in the sense that we exist in an elusive present torn between past and future and that only by predicating our predicament are we able to construct a concept of ourselves in flux or chaos.

II

Denying that the past has valuable significance for us and indicting it for the dangers, troubles, and injustices we find ourselves confronting, a great deal of poetry that has appeared in the wake of the horror of World War II has been antitraditional. Out of and around this poetry a poetics has been formed. This poetics calls for a poetry that celebrates exclusively the instant of happening, the now. In such a view, being in *place*, not in time, is what is meaningful and proper. Ironically, this poetry and poetics themselves grow out of a tradition, out of their own past, although perhaps they fail to do complete justice to the ideas of those they claim as forebears. The line of descent, however, is clear.

Ralph Waldo Emerson, for example, in "Self-Reliance," admonishes: "Speak your latent conviction, and it shall be universal sense"; and in the 1836 "Nature," he asks rhetorically, "Why should we also not enjoy an original relation to the universe?" He then answers, "The sun shines today also." In his famous open letter to Emerson, prefaced to the second edition of *Leaves of Grass*, Walt Whitman declares: "Old forms, old poems, majestic and proper in their own lands, in this land are exiles; the air here is very strong." From Whitman the line descends to William Carlos Williams, who in a letter to Robert Creeley writes: "Bad art is . . . that which does not serve in the continual service of the cleansing of all fixations upon dead, stinking dead, usages of the past." Thence to the Black Mountain School, chief guru of whom is Charles Olson, who in "Human Universe" assures us:

"If there is any absolute, it is never more than this one, you, this instant, in action." The San Francisco or Beat poets and on into a great deal of contemporary American poetry is Allen Ginsberg, for example, in "Prose Contribution to Cuban Revolution," who somewhat ungrammatically declares: "various basic rules have evolved, as far as my instincts and feelings, which are that all creation & poesy as transmission of the message of eternity is sacred and must be free of any rational restrictiveness; because consciousness has no limitations." Such self-entrancement propels the San Francisco poet Michael McClure so deeply into his phylogenetic history that, in "Phi Upsilon Kappa" [fu(c)k or puk(e)], he can confidently report the experience in which "I saw my soul and found that I lived once before and that I had been a killer whale." Or to cite another instance, what Beat poet Robin Blaser calls "personalism" leads him to report, in "The Fire": "If you imagine, as I do, that, at any evoking moment, you are a corpuscle in the left wrist of God, then any reality is precisely to be found in the flow of corpuscles in that vast body."

Granted, I have followed the line of the poetry of the moment onto a rather eccentric tangent. Yet, without veering into such extremities, I find that a great deal of poetry produced in this generation derives from the working of but half of the force of what makes poetry: from only the immediate experience of the single self.

There can be no doubt the poet needs to sharpen his or her vision in the light of each new day. Without doubt he or she needs to invigorate himself by breathing in the strong air of the place he finds him- or herself in at the moment. To be sure, he or she needs to keep the language of poetry alive by constantly recreating it. However, if what is made is to be more than private reports of experience, whether so solipsistically mystical as Robin Blaser's or so individually prosaic as my shopping list, there must be another, an opposing force. The opposition creates tension. In language it enacts our fundamental situation. We are creatures of predicament. Into presentness, gnawing it so thin it seems not to exist, are the snouts of the insatiable past and the greedy future. Poetry, I do believe, is more than self-enchantment or one-dimensional reportage.

Behind the poetics of the moment there lies, I think, a model that derives from the life sciences, more specifically from ecology. The vision of this poetry, its ideal, is one of organisms in a meadow or marsh where life, without "was" or "will be," only "is," and is in balance. Each organism exists by willing itself, that is, is "authentic," and each performs its function, that is, is "doing its thing." Symbiosis, not conflict, cooperation, not competition, prevail. All is harmony.

Appealing as it is, I have some trouble accepting the model. In one sense it is idyllic, pastoral, the Garden of Eden or Golden Age myth in a new guise. To be sure, it would be wonderful to be the first poet, to write before language was worn and contaminated. "And whatsoever Adam called every living creature, that was the name thereof," we are told in the second chapter of Genesis. Yet ours is not that opportunity or responsibility; inheriting a language, we cannot write the first poem over and over. Innocence is not given; it must be won. Language is not pure; it must be redeemed.

We might say that the Adam myth is a temporally reductive account of the birth of our linguistic capacity, of our consciousness, of a literary tradition. Here we find ourselves placed in predicament. After the birth of language, consciousness, and tradition, we exist in a tension between our inheritance *and* our always-opening-into-the-future present. In The Anxiety of Influence, Professor Harold Bloom argues that this situation generates an oedipal-like anxiety in those who make poems and guarantees misreading in those who read poems. Like the poetics and the poetry of the moment, Professor Bloom's account, it seems to me, considers only half the process, the other half. If the hold of the past on what we do *does* provoke the unconscious anguish Professor Bloom finds, the consciousness of our unfolding opportunity offers the possibility of some release from that anxiety. Every new poem is not merely a rewriting of a past poem; it is the past poem refracted or reconstructed by the novel, individual experience of the poet as well.

Might it be that the ecological model for the poetry of the moment is based on a questionable analogy? We *have* learned a great deal about the marvelous but precarious balance of life in a given environment. We well know that, while we observe, study, extrapolate from the interacting of living organisms, we, too, in the largest sense, are within such a cycle and balance. Certainly what we learn here should be critically made use of in defining ourselves and understanding our behavior as biological organisms. Yet to construct a poetic, or an ethos, on the crude wholesale application of the ecological model to ourselves as cultural, historical, conscious, and moral beings, seems to me to be as dangerous as using biological catchwords like "struggle for existence" and "survival of the fittest" as a model for constructing and justifying an unrestrainedly competitive and ruthlessly oppressive economic system and ethos. I wonder whether the ecological model is any more reliable than Social Darwinism. To consider the mutually altruistic relationship between the egret and the cow as a sanction for harmony that arises by being authentically yourself and doing your thing does strike me as being a bit naive. Is it cynical to ask about the flies that while trying to feed off the back of the cow are being eaten by the egret?

III

"Ah self, self, self. At every turn nothing but self!" cries Charles Dickens's Martin Chuzzlewit in anguish. With his compulsion to be authentic and to express his or her immediate self, the poet of the moment does perhaps run the risk of appearing narcissistic or solipsistic. As commonly applied to the making of poetry, the phrase "self-expression" might well beg the question: Which self? Or what is the self? That is the question.

Indeed, we may doubt the very existence of a concept of the self as existing before or outside of language. It would seem that the struggle to write the poem is the process of giving identity to the self. In *I and Thou*, Martin Buber writes: "in truth language does not reside in man but man stands in language and speaks out of it." Lacking an operating sense of the other, of a "before" and a "to come" as opposed to the supposed "now," of a "there" as opposed to "here," of a "not self" as opposed to "self," much of the poetry of the moment does seem to me to be self-imprisoned.

On the other hand, the poetry of tradition depends upon an operating sense of the other. In "For Bernard Shaw," Argentinian Jorge Luis Borges insists that "a book is more than a verbal structure, or a series of verbal structures; a book is a dialogue with the reader." The reader may be thought of as a predicated other, like the poet and the future. Theologian Paul Tillich advances the notion that the more nonbeing we mortal creatures are able to take into our being, the stronger our affirmation of our being becomes. So, I suggest, it is with otherness.

In reading a poem, imaginations can and do come together, however imperfectly. They do so by agreeing not on ultimate, authoritative, self-contained significations but on contingent, temporary, relative, contextual meanings. True, we must settle for what we can do as writer and can get as reader, which is always less than we crave. Yet with all its limitations and misdirections, the engagement of imaginations does provide a means for trying to escape from the black box, or cave or hole, of the immediate self, of struggling to move toward otherness, of enriching the moment with past and to come. If we decline to do and take what we can, qualified and imperfect as meaning might be, we are limited and impoverished. No need for the deconstructionists to tell us we are alone; that silence and nothingness are out there; that we come and go ultimately in separateness. Between the absolutes, about which we can do nothing, it is the struggle to be in touch, imagination to imagination, self to other, that energizes art.

In such a view, the poetic or imaginative act is not merely the assertion or expression of the immediate aspect of the being we offhandedly call our self. Quite the contrary. It is the exorcism of such a psychic construct in order to discover what Emily Dickinson calls "the self behind the self" and "the columnar self." Here, beyond the superficial, we find our deepest self. It is here we join with others in community of being. In literature the means by which we exorcize the disposable self in the discipline demanded by convention and form, the poetics that have been evolving between Adam and us. The act of writing is an opposition, an otherness which the poet must come to terms with. Against it, the force of the poet's own vision of the world and of her deep self is pushing ahead, struggling for novelty, a new birth, a won innocence. This is the poet's predicament. It is our human predicament.

Not only do language and forms evolve and grow by accretion.

The shape of human experience does too. In the literature we have inherited there are common themes and plots, myths and archetypes. It is impossible for us to wipe clean the slate of our imagination in that our listening and reading have etched these configurations of human experience into our mind. It is even true that we fit our own experience to them and within them discover its significant structures. Sometimes we resist the shapes of the past, we bend them and reshape them. Yet even when we reject them and reform them, they are exercising their force on us. So we live in a fictive tension, a fictive predicament, if you will.

No matter how novel or original our effort might seem to us formally, no matter how freshly personal the substance, what we make is to some extent informed by what our minds brings to the blank page, however reluctantly. Pure experimentation and virgin subject matter, I do believe, are illusory. Sometimes the hold of the past and the sense of the other are weak and the pull of immediacy and the sense of self are strong. Sometimes the two are quite evenly balanced in strength. Sometimes the pull of immediacy and the sense of self are weak and the hold of the past and the sense of the other are strong. The proportion varies from one literary age and generation to another. The neoclassicals were held powerfully by the past and outside authority. The romantics were tugged furiously by novelty and the ego. Even in the same writer at one time or another the proportionate strength of the grasp and pull will vary.

In our recognition, pursuit, and use of otherness, whether the otherness be a literary or cultural tradition, or formal means, or a predicated reader, we define, deal with, come to terms with the human predicament.

IV

When it comes to the making of literature, my view is not creationist but evolutionary. I do believe that a body of literature accretes by feeding both on past literature and on the nourishment of fresh experience.

Take the Troy story. We know that the poet for whom we use the name Homer did not merely report a war, nor did he simply make up a tale of two cities. Rather, he inherited stories, from an oral tradition almost surely, about an event from centuries before which, by his time, had become obscurely transformed. Then he fused these narratives with his own experience in shaping the *Iliad* and the *Odyssey*, if he, or she, composed them both. Virgil made similar use of these epics and other Troy materials and so did Chaucer and Shakespeare.

A hundred and fifty years ago, Alfred, Lord Tennyson appropriated the prophecy of Teiresias in the place of the dead, in the *Odyssey*, and a brief Christian improvisation on classical materials by Dante in Canto XXVI of the *Inferno*. Tennyson's "Ulysses" picks up the story of the Greek hero upon his return to his home in Ithaca after a twenty-year absence, then extends it. Ulysses, or Odysseus, must set out again.

Ulysses

It little profits that an idle king,
By this still hearth, among these barren crags,
Matched with an aged wife, I mete and dole
Unequal laws unto a savage race,
That hoard, and sleep, and feed, and know not me.
I cannot rest from travel; I will drink
Life to the lees. All times I have enjoyed
Greatly, have suffered greatly, both with those
That loved me, and alone; on shore, and when
Through scudding drifts the rainy Hyades
Vext the dim sea. I am become a name;
For always roaming with a hungry heart
Much have I seen and known—cities of men
And manners, climates, councils, government,
Myself not least, but honored of them all;
And drunk delight of battle with my peers,
Far on the ringing plains of windy Troy.
I am a part of all that I have met;
Yet all experience in an arch wherethrough
Gleams that untravelled world whose margin fades
For ever and for ever when I move.
How dull it is to pause, to make an end,
To rust unburnished, not to shine in use!
As though to breathe were life! Life piled on life

Were all too little, and of one to me
Little remains; but every hour is saved
From that eternal silence, something more,
A bringer of new things; and vile it were
For some three suns to store and hoard myself,
And this grey spirit yearning in desire
To follow knowledge like a sinking star,
Beyond the utmost bound of human thought.
   This is my son, mine own Telemachus,
To whom I leave the scepter and the isle—
Well-loved of me, discerning to fulfill
This labor, by slow prudence to make mild
A rugged people, and through soft degrees
Subdue them to the useful and the good.
Most blameless is he, centered in the sphere
Of common duties, decent not to fail
In offices of tenderness, and pay
Meet adoration to my household gods,
When I am gone. He works his work, I mine.
   There lies the port; the vessel puffs her sail;
There gloom the dark, broad seas. My mariners,
Souls that have toiled, and wrought, and thought with me—
That ever with a frolic welcome took
The thunder and the sunshine, and opposed
Free hearts, free foreheads—you and I are old;
Old age hath yet his honor and his toil.
Death closes all; but something ere the end,
Some work of noble note, may yet be done,
Not unbecoming men that strove with Gods.
The lights begin to twinkle from the rocks;
The long day wanes; the slow moon climbs; the deep
Moans round with many voices. Come, my friends,
'Tis not too late to seek a newer world.
Push off, and sitting well in order smite
The sounding furrows; for my purpose holds
To sail beyond the sunset, and the baths
Of all the western stars, until I die.
It may be that the gulfs will wash us down;
It may be we shall touch the Happy Isles,
And see the great Achilles, whom we knew.
Though much is taken, much abides; and though
We are not now that strength which in old days
Moved earth and heaven, that which we are, we are—

> One equal temper of heroic hearts,
> Made weak by time and fate, but strong in will
> To strive, to seek, to find, and not to yield.

While using a situation from the traditional narrative, Tennyson transforms Ulysses from the Homeric hero, the Virgilian villain, the Christian sinner Dante made him, into a great-hearted, strong-willed Victorian, who, even at the cost of abandoning wife, son, and people, must lead his devoted followers to press on and on and on. Teleology, a belief in progress, the concept of aristocratic leadership, faith in the heroic self are all coded into Tennyson's poem.

At least most Victorians so read the poem. A hundred and fifty years of intervening inhuman human history make Tennyson's Ulysses's affirmations ring a bit hollow in our ears. Underneath the optimism we sense disillusion; in the urge to sail on we detect some desire to leave this world; beneath the heroic profession we hear the plaintive cry of Thanatos. Tennyson's Ulysses is Homer's Ulysses and he is not.

Written fifty years ago, Wallace Stevens's "The World as Meditation" also jumps off from the story of Odysseus's return and retells it from the point of view of the waiting Penelope. In contrast to the assurance of Homer's faithful, devoted, watchful, suspicious wife, who demands and receives proof of the identity of the come-back king and husband, Stevens's Penelope is infected by the twentieth-century disease of doubt.

The World as Meditation

> J'ai passé trop de temps
> à travailler mon violon,
> à voyager. Mais l'exercice
> essentiel du compositeur—
> la méditation—rien ne l'a
> jamais suspendu en moi. . . .
> Je vis un rêve permanent,
> qui ne s'arrête ni nuit
> ni jour.
> —Georges Enesco

Is it Ulysses that approaches from the east,
The interminable adventurer? The trees are mended.
That winter is washed away. Someone is moving.

On the horizon and lifting himself up above it.
A form of fire approaches the cretonnes of Penelope,
Whose mere savage presence awakens the world in which she dwells.

She has composed, so long, a self with which to welcome him,
Companion to his self for her, which she imagined,
Two in a deep-founded sheltering, friend and dear friend.

The trees had been mended, as an essential exercise
In an inhuman meditation, larger than her own.
No winds like dogs watched over her at night.

She wanted nothing he could bring her by coming alone.
She wanted no fetchings. His arms would be her necklace
And her belt, the final fortune of their desire.

But was it Ulysses? Or was it only the warmth of the sun
On her pillow? The thought kept beating in her like her heart.
The two kept beating together. It was only day.

It was Ulysses and it was not. Yet they had met,
Friend and dear friend and a planet's encouragement.
The barbarous strength within her would never fail.

She would talk a little to herself as she combed her hair,
Repeating his name with its patient syllables,
Never forgetting him that kept coming constantly so near.

Penelope has waited so long and wished so hard for Ulysses's return that she may be imposing the shape of her own mind on the man who claims to be her husband or who may be still another imposter. Even if the man is Ulysses, he is not only the Ulysses who left her for Troy twenty years ago. He is twenty years of another man as well. Just as in the poem Penelope says to herself, "It was Ulysses and it was not," we say about Penelope, it is Homer's Penelope and it is not.

In Stevens's poem we find a tensed fusing of a traditional story and theme—the return in disguise of the king and lover—with the sensibility of modern Western humanity. The poem is charged with a skepticism that is both existential and dramatic. The idiom of the poem is that of the post-symbolist, modern poet, itself full of uncertainty. In reading the poem we experience an enactment in language of the human predicament: the old against the new, the inherited against the innovative, assurance against doubt, traditional conventions against the individual genius of the contemporary poet. And what Stevens has made of the Odysseus myth affects our reading of Homer. As Borges puts it in his essay on Nathaniel Hawthorne: "a great writer creates his precursors. He creates and somehow justifies them."

In a poem entitled "The Return," within a section of a volume significantly entitled "Retellings," I too have been engaged by the crisis of Odysseus' homecoming and I also attempt an improvisation on it.

The Return

Home was a flop. The woman flatulent
and fat, wedded to a half-filled bed.

Before my eyes, the bitch, pig from a pup,
heaved to her feet, grunted once, rolled dead.

Well on his way back to boy, my father
imagined his arm could sling a spear.
It aroused a guffaw.

And my son, dear Goddess! a man
yet not a man, female infected, butt
of men's jibes, dreamer and dodger—phew!
unable to string a bow.

My beautiful people—palsied or gone
into shades. Their vulture sons,
pecking each other's eyes while I was gone—
a phalanx of beaks within the eagle's nest.

Over the palace, moss everywhere.
Weary my brain, fevered by songs
of swallows following from the south.

    Now sail is set, the tiller steady.
    This time my own skiffsman.

> Wind sputters, coughs, chokes on itself.
> Wonderful through this calm those voices close.
>
> Scars of the hawsers they'd braceleted my wrists
> and ankles with tell the whole story.

Here I, too, wish to do something more than rehearse the traditional tale. While counting on the narratives being familiar, I endeavor to refract or reconstruct the old experience so that the light it sheds, if any, will make us see the theme of the returned warrior in a new way.

The idiom of my poem is not that of Tennyson's or Stevens's. My Odysseus opens his monologue by declaring "Home was a flop." After a second world war, in which two cities were atomized and how many others incinerated, followed by a number of deadly aftermaths euphemistically called "dirty little wars," a number of genocides, those who return can scarcely expect their homecomings to be triumphant and sweet. The language, like the experience, is debased from Homer and Virgil's formal poetry, from Chaucer's flexible and fluent rhyme royal, from the rich blank verse of Shakespeare, from the slightly stilted eloquence of Tennyson, from the deliberately uncertain, controlledly vague, engagingly suggestive manner of Stevens.

The scarcely elevated word "flop" is meant to contain and to characterize the catalog of disappointments the warrior king's homecoming is: no welcome from his queen and one-time lover, whose beauty and desire have departed ("The woman flatulent / and fat, wedded to a half-filled bed"); the grotesque aging ("pig from a pup") and inopportune death of his dog; the loss of puissance and dignity in his father (the old man's effort to throw a spear provokes a guffaw); the lack of promise in his feckless son ("dreamer and dodger"); the corruption and faithlessness of his subjects (the old are "palsied," the young confront him in his own home as "a phalanx of beaks"); the decay of his palace ("moss everywhere"). Did he do something wrong?

As Homer's Teiresias foretells and as Dante's Ulysses in Hell reports, my Odysseus, like Tennyson's Ulysses, chooses to set forth again. In that moment of crisis, when he must decide, Odysseus, like the poem and like us, is at once gripped by the awful past he has returned from, constrained by the limitations and disappointments of his present, and pulled by an imagined future. Unlike Tennyson's Victorian hero, my life-sized protagonist does not rally his mariner followers to set sail so that under his indomitable leadership they together may perform "some work of noble note" and strive and seek and find "a newer world." Come back from his war, the war of Auschwitz and Hiroshima, weary and disillusioned, my Odysseus can find no sanction for a belief in progress, for any expectation of triumphant achievement, for any faith in himself to master life.

The title, which in essence is the poem, doubles back on itself. The return from war was a flop; the battered heartsick soldier and sailor in one decides to make another return, to turn back. In his inner ear, above the farting, grunting, guffawing, even above the still-heard detonations and the cries of suffering and dying from the war, he hears the song of the Sirens, or "sea girls, wreathed with seaweed red and brown," whom he, as T. S. Eliot's J. Alfred Prufrock could not, had heard singing to him when he was tied to the mast of his duty by the hawser of responsibility. Note here the pulling into the present moment of consciousness of the poem Eliot the Modernist, Tennyson the Victorian, Dante the medieval Christian, and Homer the ancient Hellene. All of this tradition is pertinent, but the poem projects itself beyond its precursors.

Caught between the still vivid reality of the butchery of a war and the present dissension he confronts, the contemporary Odysseus has driven home to him the awful truth that community has been broken. He must make his return from his return alone ("This time my own skiffsman."). The nature and value and ramifications of his quest for pure peace and uncorrupted beauty are problematical. Pursuit of these ideals, he seems to know, might cost him his life's breath (wind "chokes on itself"). On his wrists and ankles he carries admonitory scars, reminding him of the price he already has had to pay for merely a fleeting experience with that compelling beauty. His final words declare that he bears the stigmata of suffering.

He is Odysseus and he is not. Referentially within him is a long past, a tradition of heroism and faith. But now he is changed. He has been part of organized inhumanity and destruction. He has experienced the breaking of community. Faith has betrayed him. He has lost belief. His gods are dead. Here is a momentous predicament, a soul-shattering, moral collision. As our Odysseus chooses to return from his return to a vision that already has hurt and scarred him, and might well cost him his life, as the poem falls into itself, so to speak, we are projected into the uncertainty of the future.

"Who can deny that things to come are not yet? Yet already there is in mind an expectation of things to come," writes St. Augustine. As we leave the poem, in which past, present, and future are compressed into a single tension, enacting the larger predicament in which all of us find ourselves, we must make what we can and will of the one who is Odysseus and is not, who is not us and is.